Anonymous

Prison Life in Texas

Anonymous

Prison Life in Texas

ISBN/EAN: 9783744759274

Printed in Europe, USA, Canada, Australia, Japan

Cover: Foto ©ninafisch / pixelio.de

More available books at **www.hansebooks.com**

PRISON LIFE IN TEXAS

AN ACCOUNT

OF

HE CAPTURE, AND IMPRISONMENT

OF A PORTION OF THE

46th Regiment Indiana Veteran Volunteers,

IN TEXAS·

JOURNAL OFFICE, LOGANSPORT, INDIANA.

ADVERTISEMENT.

This narrative is the experience of a portion of the 46th Regiment, Indiana Veteran Volunteers, as prisoners at Camps Ford and Groce, Texas.

Although there were many noble representatives of other Regiments and States, in those places of torture, no want of consideration for them, will be charged in omitting more particular mention of them. The work is designed, more especially, as a regimental history, in which the privations and sufferings of a part of the men may be had in a tangible form, for the satisfaction of the prisoners, their comrades and friends.

THE RED RIVER EXPEDITION.

In December, 1863, an expedition was fitted out at New Orleans, under Major General Banks against Texas, and in conjunction with one under General Steele, against the whole trans-Mississippi Department of the Rebel Government.

The objective point of this expedition was Galveston, or Sabine City, which it was proposed to reach through the Teche and Bayou Beof countries, by Franklin, Oppelousas, Alexandria and Nachitoches—on by Shreveport, across the Sabine River, and south to the point determined upon. The column of General Steele, was expected to meet that of General Banks, at Shreveport.

Nothing was spared to make the expedition certain. The Commissary, Quarter-Master, and Ordnance Departments, furnishes material in the most lavish manner, and nothing seemed wanting but courage, endurance, and good management on the campaign, to ensure its success. The troops forming the expedition, had, the most of them, been in the service over two years, and upon many fields and campaigns had proven their courage and endurance. The reputation of General Banks, guaranteed the generalship.

From New Orleans there went the 13th and 19th Army Corps. Of the former, there were but two divisions present—the 3d and 4th. The 1st and 2d were at Brownsville, Texas. Of the 3d division, the 11th, 24th, 34th and 47th Indiana regiments, were home on Veteran furlough—thus reducing the division far below the mininum. This corps was under the command of General Ransom. The 19th was commanded by General Franklin.

A fleet of gunboats and monitors, under Commander Porter, passed up Red River, and was expected to reduce the forts and batteries along the banks of the river, and keep open the communication with the Mississippi.

From Vicksburg there was sent the 16th Army Corps, under General A. J. Smith, which went up Red River on transports.

The entire expedition started in good time. That portion which left Vicksburg, encountered the rebels at Fort De Russey, and there achieved a splendid victory. The fort was carried by a brilliant movement, and a number of guns and prisoners taken. A large amount of cotton fell into the hands of the Navy.

The corps and navy then passed on up the river. The former joined General Banks at Pleasant Hill, the day after the victory gained by the rebels had settled the expedition. The fleet with an infantry force under General Kilby Smith, went on up towards Shreveport, and was many miles above "Grand Ecore," when the retreating Federal army reached that point, on the road back. The capture of the fleet and troops above, seemed inevitable, but as the expedition was running on luck, rather than management, they escaped with but little loss.

That portion of the column in which was the 46th Indiana, left Algiers, March 6th. The following, a brief diary of the march, will be interesting to those who were in the expedition :

March 6th.   Left Algiers, arrived at " Brashear City " and crossed " Berwick Bay " same evening.

7th to 12th.   In camp.

13th.   Marched sixteen miles to Boreland's Platation.

14th.   Five miles beyond Franklin.

15th.   In camp.

16th.   Marched to within six miles of New Iberia.

17th.   Seventeen miles to Spanish Lake.

18th.   Fifteen miles to Vermillion Bayou.

19th.   To Camp Fair View, near Grand Coteau, eighteen miles.

20th. Eighteen miles, to a point two miles beyond Washington. Camped on "Bayou Cortableaux."

21st. In camp.

22d. Sixteen miles, and encamped on " Bayou Beof."

23d. Twenty-three miles. Still on " Bayou Beof."

24th. Marched twelve miles. Encamped near a Steam Saw Mill.

25th. Fourteen miles. Honored a rebel Captain's plantation with a camp.

26th. Six miles beyond Alexandria, on the "Bayou Rapids."

27th. In camp. The cavalry routed the enemy and captured some prisoners.

28th. Very rainy. Eighteen miles on the "Bayou Rapids."

29th. Fifteen miles. Encamped on Big Cane.

30th. In camp.

31st. Sixteen miles. on " Little Cane."

April 1st. To Nachitoches, twenty-two miles.

2d to 5th. In camp in rear of the town.

6th. Fifteen miles to " Oak Bottoms."

7th. To " Pleasant Hill," twenty miles.

8th. Fifteen miles to " Sabine Cross Roads," where the battle was fought. Divisions were sent in only as fast as the rebels could dispose of them. Returned to " Pleasant Hills," which was reached at 4 next morning.

9th. The 16th Corps came up. Battle of " Pleasant Hills." Beat the rebels off, but started for the river. Marched until 3 next morning.

10th. Started at 5 A. M., and arrived at " Oak Bottom" at noon.

11th. Left at 4:30 A. M., and arrived at " Grand Ecore," at noon.

12th. Work on entrenchments. Reports of attack. Portions of our army hurrying in.

13th and 14th. Work on entrenchment. Reports of rebels coming to attack. Bad news from the gunboats above.

15th. Great excitement about the fleet above.

16th to 21st. Still at "Grand Ecore." Rebels watching and waiting for us to move. Fleet comes down. Receive orders to march at 5 P. M. All ready but did not start until 2:30 next morning. Meanwhile, town caught fire.

22d. Marched until 2 o'clock next morning.

23d. Started at 6 A. M. Reached "Big Cane." Also the rebels. Battle. Rebels on front and rear. Beat them off, and traveled.

24th. Left "Big Cane" at 8 A. M., and marched to "Bayou Rapids," eighteen miles.

25th. Eighteen miles, to within two miles of "Alexandria." Very hot and dusty.

26th. In camp. Work on entrenchments.

27th. First Division of the 13th Army Corps arrives from Texas.

28th. Ordered to attack the enemy. Did so and came back.

29th and 30th. In camp. Very hot. Working on the dam. 47th Indiana arrived.

May 1st. In line of battle all the time. Rebels inquisitive. They get below on the river.

2d. Ordered to go out after the enemy. Skirmished all day. Rebels followed back, and threw shell into camp. Transport "Emma" captured below and burned.

3d. Very hot. In line of battle all day. Rebels in view. Heavy rumors. River open but lined with rebels. "Rob Roy" arrived from below. Work on dam progressing. The river and the expedition dam—ed by the army.

4th. Entrenching. Cannonading down the river. "City Belle," with the 120th Ohio, captured. Boat burned and Colonels Mudd, Bassett, and Speegle, killed. 56th Ohio start home on the "Warner" on "veteran" furlough.

5th. Marched out. Fought the rebels all day. Sharp shelling. Steamer "Warner" was captured. Many of the regiment killed and wounded. Transport and Gunboats "18" and "25," burned. "Veteran furloughs" at a discount.

6th. Marched out at noon. Skirmished all the afternoon. Went five miles. Laid all night at "Middle Bayou" in line of battle.

7th. Started at 6 A. M. Went forward. Met the enemy at once. Skirmished all day. Arrived at "Bayou Rapids Bridge" at 5 P. M. Drove the rebels across. Major McNiel, of Texas, caught sneaking around the skirmish line and shot. Had $700 in rebel money and important papers in his pocket. Left at 10 P. M., and fell back to last night's position.

8th to 12th. In line of battle at "Middle Bayou," keeping the rebels back whilst the dam is being built. All kinds of weather. Corn over a foot high. Rebels keep us busy. Heavy explosion about Alexandria. Many rumors.

13th. Ordered to leave at sunrise. Started at 2:30 P. M. Struck the river some miles below Alexandria after dark. River crowded with boats. The lights looked like those of a city.

14th. Started at 6 A. M. Slow marching. Troops take the levee ; the wagons the road. Hot and dusty. Halted at 12 midnight. Food and fodder scarce. Burning buildings on the right, in front and rear. Men very tired.

15th. Started at 7 A. M. Went one mile and a half by 3:30 P. M. Attack on the rear. Rebels shell sharply. Drove them back. Head of column building bridge over Bayou Chateau. Marched at 3:30 P. M. Made twelve miles by 1:30 next morning. Road full of refugees on carts, wagons, foot and horse-back. Many wagons burned.

16th. Laid down in line of battle at 1:30 A. M. Ordered to move at 3. Started at 4. Met the enemy at 7. Formed lines. Rebel lines a mile and a half long. Drove them. Battles of Marksville and Mansura. Towns heavily visited. Reports of much confiscation and burning. Started again at 2 P. M. Halted in the bed of a Bayou at 4:30 P. M.

17th. Started at 2:30 A. M. Went six miles by 5:30. Halted two hours, and reached and crossed "Bayou Glaze" by 5 o'clock. Rebel attack on rear and front. Drove them back. Very oppressive weather.

18th. Awaiting the building of a pontoon over the Atchafalya. Rebels in heavy force attacked General Mower's two brigades, on the east of the Bayou. About 15,000 men stood and looked on whilst 8,000 rebels fought 4,000 of our troops. Regiments all ready to fall in, but no orders. Watched the fight three hours, when the rebels retired. Our loss 600. Rebels over 1,000.

19th. Orders to flank the rebels. Made the movement down the "Atchafalya," but no rebels there. Returned to the big pontoon at 4 P. M.

20th. Crossed the pontoon built of steam-boats. Marched up the Atchafalya and waited for the column. At 5 the bridge was broken up and the boats, at high speed, went towards Red River and the Mississippi. Column started at 11 P. M.

21st. Halted at 8 A. M. for breakfast. Reached the Mississippi at 10 A. M. Marched down it and halted at 7:30 P. M.

22nd. Started at 3:30 A. M., and reached Morganza at 1 P. M.

Battle of Mansfield.

On the night of the 7th of April, 1864, the entire infantry force of the army encamped at Pleasant Hill, nineteen miles from Mansfield. The cavalry, near this point, having overtaken the rear guard of the enemy, under General Green, after a brief skirmish, drove the rebel force forward, killing thirty and wounding sixty men. General Lee's loss being twenty killed and fifty wounded. The cavalry then moved on about six miles, and went into camp for the night. The infantry force mentioned, was now well concentrated and in high spirits. The baggage and supply trains were all up, and the artillery was conveniently parked. Long lines of camp-fires gleamed brightly through the thick pine forest. Groops of dusty men, with high hopes sang patriotic songs around blazing pine faggots, whilst others reposed on the soft carpet of leaves, dreaming of home and those who were there watching for their return, little thinking that the next night would find them hurrying to the same spot, broken and scattered; with many lying stiff in death, or with mangled limbs, in the hands of a heartless and exasperated foe. But a happy joyous night was soon to be turned to mourning.

On the 8th the sun rose bright in a cloudless sky, ushering in a beautiful, but to the Union army a disastrous day. At 5 o'clock, the 4th Division of the 13th Army Corps, commanded by Colonel Landrum, of the 19th Kentucky, numbering about eighteen hundred men, moved forward to support the cavalry. At 6 o'clock, the 3d Division of the 13th Corps, under command of Brigadier General R. A. Cameron, numbering, exclusive of train-guards, about twelve hundred, followed. The 13th Corps was under command of Brigadier General Ransom.

After this force came the supply and ammunition trains of the 13th Corps. The trains of the cavalry were all in front.

At 7 o'clock General Emory, with one division of the 19th Corps, moved in rear of the trains of the 13th Corps, who was followed by the whole train of the army, except the portions specified as going before. The remainder of the 19th Corps, which was the bulk of the army, followed under Major General Franklin.

The train numbered over six hundred wagons, of which those of the General's staff formed no inconsiderable portion.

The road over which this enormous train was to pass was a narrow, tortuous passage, through a dense pine forest—so narrow in many places, that a single horseman could scarcely pass the moving wagons. The rear-guard of the army did not get away from camp until after 12 o'clock.

At this time the 16th Corps, under General A. J.

Smith, was on the road from Grand Ecore, where it had disembarked from boats.

About 7 o'clock, the cavalry discovered the enemy, about 5,000 strong, strongly posted on a deep Bayou, about eight miles from "Pleasant Hill." A brisk skirmish ensued,—on our side principally with carbines,—our cavalry being dismounted, the nature of the ground forbidding the cavalry movements, and permitting but a few pieces of artillery to be used. The 4th Division was at once hurried forward and the enemy was speedily dislodged and driven away. The contest here was brief, but fierce. The enemy fell back, slowly and stubbornly contesting the ground, and closely pursued by the cavalry and the small body of infantry. A running fight was kept up for a distance of eight miles, when at 2 o'clock, the enemy, after passing a plantation of some six hundred acres, made a determined stand.

A council of war was now held by General Banks, at which all the Generals of divisions were present. It was proposed to go into camp, issue rations, and give the 19th and 16th Corps time to come up, and be prepared on the next morning to fight the battle which appeared imminent. This wise proposition was over-ruled, and General Lee was ordered to push the enemy. It was argued that the enemy was not in force in front, but that it was nothing more than the force that had been opposing the expedition for the day or two previous, and that the cavalry, supported by the infantry, then up, was sufficient for the work.

During this halt the 3d Division had moved up to within four miles of the scene of action. Whilst the consultation was going on, it was ordered to go into camp. It remained at this point about two hours, when General Cameron received orders to move at once to the front.

By this time the battle raged furiously. It was found that the entire rebel force was in position, behind hastily constructed works of logs. The cavalry had broken and fell in disorder back. The cavalry train was halted in the road, blocking it up against the advance of artillery, and preventing the mass of retreating horsemen from escaping, but through the lines of infantry. The 4th Division fought with desperation. The rebel lines were forced, only to give way again before them. It had to oppose the entire rebel army and the struggle was decided by numbers. But eighteen hundred men, (with a very small portion of cavalry) were engaged on the Union side in this contest.

The Union lines being comparatively short, the extended lines of the enemy were enabled to close around this small force, and the retreat of a large portion was cut off. The cavalry stampeded, leaving infantry, artillery and train at the mercy of the enemy. The infantry cut through to find itself again surrounded. The ammunition after two hours hard fighting, was exhausted, and a surrender was unavoidable.

Such was the condition of affairs when General Cameron arrived on the ground with the 3d Division, numbering not over twelve hundred men. Line of battle was immediately formed with the 1st Brigade, (composed of the 46th Indiana and five companies of the 29th Wisconsin, under Lieutenant Colonel A. M. Flory,) on the right, and the 2d Brigade, (composed of the 24th and 28th Iowa, and the 56th Ohio, under Lieutenant Colonel Raynor,) on the left. The position of the division was on the edge of a wood, with the open plantation in front. It was about three-fourths of a mile across, with nothing to obstruct the view, but an occasional swell of the ground. The width of this open space was more than thrice the length of the front of the 2d Division, now the only troops left to confront the enemy.

The rebels, elated with their late success, came pouring over the clearing, in successive lines, with closely massed columns. They were permitted to come within close musket range, before the 3d Division opened upon them. The Union position was such that, concealed behind logs and fences, it could not be accurately ascertained by the rebels, giving an unusually fine opportunity for deliberate and accurate firing. A deadly volley broke forth

from the whole line—breaking the rebel ranks, hurling
them back in confusion, and leaving the ground strewn
with their dead and wounded. The rattle of the deadly
muskets was unceasing, and the rebel slaughter was terrible.

The enemy rapidly retreated, but again reformed heavi-
er lines, with fresh troops. Now was the time for the
19th Corps to have been brought up, and forming on the
right and left of the line, already there, prevented the
flanking by the enemy, through which they gained their
victory. But that was not the arrangement. The 19th
Corps was some four miles in the rear, in camp, and
could not be brought up until the 3d, like the 4th Division, had been sacrificed.

The rebels advanced again and again, but could not
maintain themselves upon the ground. They were driv-
en back—lines, numbering not less than eight thousand,
by this little force of twelve hundred.

Another, but feebler demonstration, was made on the
front by a small part of the enemy, whilst the bulk of
the force, under cover of the woods, on either side, passed around to the flanks and rear of the Union lines.
This closed the contest. The 3d Division was surrounded. It maintained the line, and endeavored to fall back,
but the rebels, coming actually among the men, forced
them to break, to enable the few that might, to escape.
The men fought to the last moment, and continued firing
until forced to cease by capture, or by the want of amu-
nition. They fought from tree to tree, pursued by the
rebel cavalry, a mile and a half, when a portion of the
19th Corps coming up, saved the remnant, not killed or
captured.

The 19th Corps drove back the rebels with considerable slaughter, and night coming on ended the conflict for
the day.

The cavalry train being in the road, blocked it up completely. The pine woods were so thick that artillery
could not be moved through it, so it was impossible to
bring off the wagon, artillery and ambulance trains. All

fell into the hands of the rebels. The cavalry train was heavily laden with commissary stores and officers' property, and was rich booty for the rebels.

This was the battle of "Mansfield," or "Sabine Cross Roads," where an expedition, fitted out, without regard to expense, finely appointed, in every necessary material ; with an army never before defeated—men who had stood at Vicksburg, Jackson, Port Hudson and Baton Rouge—defeated and destroyed with a loss of material inestimable, and a sacrifice of life, terrible to remember, through a plan of battle which threw into the fight detachments of troops, only as fast as they could be destroyed. Here was committed one of the great blunders of the war, and one for which nobody, as yet, has accounted.

The loss of the Union army at this battle, was six hundred killed and wounded, and twelve hundred and fifty captured. The loss of the rebels, as taken from their official reports, was thirty-one hundred, of whom, ten days after, one thousand were dead. Texas and Louisiana were in mourning for the calamity that fell upon them. Very many prominent officers were killed. General Mouton, of Louisiana, and General Green, of Texas, the hope of that part of the Confederacy, were victims. Scarcely a company came out without the loss of all, or nearly all of its commissioned officers, and the victory was more dearly paid for than would have made repetition profitable.

The March to Camp Ford.

After their capture, the prisoners were rapidly pushed to the rear. Along the road from the battle-field to Mansfield, four miles, the road was strewn with dead rebels, and the debris of the battle. The wounded were being gathered up, and the country was covered with temporary hospitals, to which the rebels were carrying their crowds of wounded.

At Mansfield, about two hundred of our prisoners were crowded into the Court House, and for the night, were confined in a room scarcely large enough for half that number. This room had been used by rebel troops for quarters, and was filled with filth and excrement; being in just such a condition as a most degraded band of savages would be likely to leave it. The rest of the prisoners were corraled on a freshly plowed field, near the town, and compelled to get what rest they might, after twenty miles' march, and two hours' hard fighting, on the ground, saturated as it was, with recent rains. Nothing, of any consequence, had been eaten since five o'clock that morning. Most of the men had lost their knapsacks in the fight, and with nothing but their clothing, hungry and tired, they began, under such circumstances, a long and torturing imprisonment. The cold, north wind chilled the blood and benumbed the bodies of the captives, and they esteemed their sufferings great, but the time was to come, when they could look back upon this night as pleasantly passed, compared with many of their experience.

On the morning of the 9th, the day after the battle, the entire capture was assembled and moved forward, towards their destination, in Texas. No rations, whatever, were issued to the prisoners. Chilled, hungry and weary, this band, numbering fifty commissioned officers and twelve hundred men, were goaded forward, between two lines of rebel cavalry, flushed with a blundering success, and void of all the principles of manhood and the honor of the soldier, and filled with a brutish ferocity, developed and sharpened by their losses and their triumph. The most insulting epithets were heaped upon these defenceless men, these prisoners, and those who, from sickness or exhaustion, reeled in the ranks, were treated only as a slave-driving chivalry can treat defenceless humanity.

At six o'clock at night, after a march of twenty-four miles, the staggering column was turned into an open field, having had an unbroken fast of two days. About ten o'clock at night, a small allowance of wood was given the prisoners. a pint of musty, unsifted corn-meal, with a small allowance of salt beef, no salt, and one baking pan to each hundred men. There was no water within a fourth of a mile. Eight or ten men were taken out at a time to fill the canteens, of which a very small number had escaped the notice of the rapacious captors on the battle-field. The entire night was spent in trying to prepare food from the scanty materials at hand—a task almost impossible.

Poetical imaginations, reveling in sumptuously filled stomachs, and cheered by a bright, blazing fire, speak of sleep as "a sweet restorer;" but a thinly clad man to woo sleep on the cold, wet ground, with the starry sky for a covering, and outside of such a supper as has been alluded to, fails, most decidedly, to see the point.

At daybreak, on the morning of the 10th, the haggard procession was again put in motion, and marched a distance of twenty-five miles. During this day's march, many men were forced along by the bayonet, and by threats of shooting.

About the same rations were issued as the evening before, with the addition of an abundant supply of water from a creek. In keeping with the consideration generally showed the prisoners, by the guards, they encamped above the prisoners, and washed the horses and their own persons in the stream, and in other ways, rendered the water as filthy, as a systematic endeavor could make it.

After marching and halting in this manner for sixteen days, the point of destination was reached. The women and children from the country, on either side of the road, for miles, congregated in motley groups to witness the imposing spectacle. The doors and windows of each house were filled with crowds of haggard women, white-headed, ragged children, and naked negroes, of all sizes and ages; old men and boys, were posting hurriedly to the front, armed with every conceivable weapon known to the gunsmith for the last century, and mounted in every imaginable style. Confederate flags were displayed in abundance; fit emblems of their treachery and villainy. In passing any considerable group, or a town, our un-

daunted heroes in blue, drowned all shouts of exultation
of the foe, with patriotic national songs. The "Rally
Round the Flag, Boys," seemed to have a new signifi·
cance, and swelling out from a thousand brave souls,
drowned the weak ebullition of rebel huzzas. Never were
the rallying songs of the nation more appropriately used,
nor with greater effect, in impressing upon the traitors an
idea of the moral force of the nation, and its inevitable
triumph.

The Rev. Hamilton Robb, Chaplain of the 46th Indiana, a man near 70 years of age, made this march, a prisoner. He was released by order of Kirby Smith, at
Camp Ford, late in June. This officer had also been captured at Champion Hill, on the Vicksburg march in 1863.

Previous to the arrival of the prisoners captured from
General Banks, Camp Ford was occupied by about eight
hundred men and officers, including one hundred and fifty
officers and sailors, captured at various points on the
coast of Texas.

The army was represented by Colonel Burrell and eight
officers of the 42d Massachusetts, who were captured at
Galveston, about the 12th of January, 1863; the enlisted men had all been paroled; the officers who were
captured at Brashear City, La., in June, 1863; the 19th
Iowa Infantry, Lieutenant Colonel Leake; the 26th Indiana, Lieutenant Colonel Rose, captured at Morganza, in
September, 1863, with other and smaller bodies of troops
of General Heron's command. Of the navy, were the
officers and crew of the "Morning Light," captured off
Sabine Pass, February 12, 1863; the officers and crews
of the "Sachem" and "Clifton," captured on the attack
on Sabine City, by General Franklin, September, 1863,
and some officers captured at Brashear City.

In April, 1864, these men were almost destitute of
clothing. Many of them at capture, were robbed of all
articles not absolutely necessary to cover their nakedness. They had passed one of the coldest winters known
in the country for years, in this destitute condition. More
than three-fourths of the men had no shoes to their feet

for months. In December they had been marched to Shreveport, a distance of one hundred and forty miles, and back again in January, through rain, snow and sleet, and over icy roads, with no shelter at night, on rations of coarse meal and starved beef. Again, in March, they were marched over the same road and again back to Camp Ford, their condition not, in the least, improved by the lapse of time.

These movements, it is said, were made for the purpose of exchange, but they were not finally released until July, when they left prison, many of them in about the condition of Adam and Eve, on their entree into society.

On the 20th of April, the prisoners captured at Pleasant Hill arrived at Camp Ford—about eight hundred—and were at once assigned quarters within its hospitable limits.

Early in May, some fifteen hundred men and officers, captured from General Steele's army in Arkansas, were added to the already overcrowded prison-pen, and at various times, the captures from transports and gunboats, until the number reached forty-eight hundred.

Steele's men were captured at Mark's Mills, Arkansas. Their treatment had been most barbarous. As soon as they had been marched to the rear, they were systematically and completely stripped of everything—hats, boots, coats, pants, shirts and drawers, and left to go naked, or put on the filthy rags thrown away by the scoundrels who had robbed them. Their money, watches, and, in short, every article in their possession, was taken from them. Even the treasured miniatures of their wives and mothers were taken and made the subjects of gross, vulgar ribaldry, then thrown into heaps, when the chivalry rode over them with their horses. At Shrevesport they were again subjected to inspection, and made to pass in single file, before a guard, so that any articles that had, by any stratagem, been concealed, might be discovered.

Camp Ford.

The prison is four miles from Tyler, Smith county, Texas. It covers an area of about six acres, enclosed by a stockade. A trench or ditch, was first dug around the ground selected; in it were placed, on end, oak or pine timbers, fitted close together, and forming a wall about eight feet high. On the outside, the earth was banked up so that the guards, whilst on their beats, could see over the whole camp. The location was on an abrupt hill-side—a kind of pine and oak barrens. Every shrub and tree was carefully cut down, leaving nothing to protect the prisoners from the drenching rains, the chilly dews of night, or the scorching rays of the semi-tropical sun. Within this pen the prisoners were turned, and mockingly told to "make yourselves comfortable."

The officers had the rare privilege granted them of going to the woods, under guard, to cut logs and board timber, which they carried in on their backs, and constructed for themselves huts for shelter. Thus, parties of five and ten going out, in due time, built up cabins, a labor not light, when it is considered that to near forty-eight hundred men, but twenty axes and four or five shovels were allowed. An auger and an old saw made up the complement of available tools. Outside, in the camps of the guards, there seemed to be abundance, but nothing but the assortment named, could be procured for the inside.

The private soldiers, with the greatest difficulty, b· ·n armful of brush, brought in one day, and some twigs the next, sought to erect shelters to protect them from the sun. Parties of from ten to twenty were successively passed out, under guard, with one or two old axes, and a short time allowed them to procure this class of material; but so great was the clamor and eager rush for the prison gate by the men, that in their ill humor, the officers in charge, for days, would all · none to go out. Hundreds of the men dug holes in the hill.side, and from two to four lived in each, like wild animals. Each rain soaked through their thin covering of earth and soon made their only abiding place untenable, even for well raised swine. Others, with little enterprise, made no efforts to construct any kind of shelter. A very large proportion, owing to the scarcity of tools, and the many impediments thrown in their way, were unable, with all their efforts, to get anything up till late in the summer. The men who lived in the caves soon became sick, and death became a frequent guest in these unnatural abodes. Many of these unfortunate men will be cripples for life from such exposure.

The only reply to complaints of such neglect, was, that "You might have stayed at home!" "You had no business to come down here and interfere with us." "We did'nt want to fight you 'uns." "If you 'uns had stayed at home, we 'uns wouldn't have interrupted you 'uns." "Good enough for you." These, to the subjects of the argument, were not very logical deductions, but unavoidable conclusions.

To add to the misery of living in such hovels, this was one of the wettest seasons Texas had witnessed for twenty years. During the entire months of May and June, and far into July, rain fell almost constantly, not figuratively, but literally, in torrents—floods overhead and cataracts under foot. With blankets, only, in the proportion of ten men to one—robbed of clothing, in many cases, these unfortunate men were compelled, almost in a state of nakedness, to endure the drenching rains, day and night. What though rain should cease, the dark gloom of a cheerless night, like some demon, would spread its impenetrable vale over the camp, and, exagerate, if possible, the misery of the sufferers. They do not freeze, but they shiver in every muscle. The body does not become numb, but there is an uneasy, unsatisfied craving for warmth, that seems worse than a positively colder degree. Men seem to draw within themselves, and shiver, as they remember the comforts of home, and would barter for the firesides of home, the entire world besides.

The ragged, haggard, careworn men, huddled together in groups, like sheep, as if to kindle a little warmth by contact, and move the blood that fast seemed ceasing to flow in their veins. So, night after night passed, of sleepless wretchedness, with no hope of comfort in the coming morn, but the warming influences of day. Many of the prisoners were new recruits on their first campaign, and unaccustomed to the exposure of even ordinary camp life. Upon these. the trial soon began to tell, and each night witnessed the death of some unfortunate man, breathing out his life in darkness. Lying in the mud, with the rain falling upon him, he becomes insensible to the loud thunder and the vivid lightning, and is beyond the reach of those who had tortured him. No mother near to gently smooth the aching brow; the kind hand of no sister to minister to his wants; no wife, with her deep love watching the spirit's last struggle.

Hurried to a near grave, scarcely deep enough to hide the body from the prowling wolf, it is soon forever disposed of.

Life Inside.

The inside of a prison camp cannot, like many other things, be imagined. It must be lived in—seen, felt—to be comprehended. Fancy and imagination, in most cases. can bring to view scenes of beauty or pictures of terror, but the degree of wretchedness in real, barbarous prison life, such as the rebel government has systematically and intentionally imposed upon its prisoners of war, is too extreme and unusual, in ordinary experience, to be appreciated anywhere outside of their infernal boundaries. Such suffering is only known by the heart throbs felt in a rebel prison, for such throbs are no where else experienced. The pen or tongue is inadequate to paint and group in one comprehensive idea, the multiplied sources of annoyance, pain and horror, that have their rise in the prisons of Southern traitors. They contain a multi-

tude of ragged, dispirited men, covered with filth, and
anxious only, about the most ordinary and primary ne-
cessities of life. Reckless, regardless of everything but
what pertains to their own immediate personal existence.
Shivering with the cold at night, and scorched by the sun
in day-time. Without hats to protect the head, or clothes
to protect the back, the elements have uninterrupted influence upon them, and becomes the fruitful source of disease and death.

Through the main street of Camp Ford, the larger portion of the prisoners passed for water, and Broadway
never presented a more busy scene of barter and traffic,
than here appeared. Nor did any "broker's board" ever
present so much intenseness as was exhibited among the
prisoners and outsiders in commercial operations. Here
was brought the produce of the surrounding country, for
sale at fabulous prices. Flour at five hundred dollars a
barrel! There was no sign of shame on the face of the
pampered slave-driver, when he demanded from the reel-
ing, exhausted prisoner, forty dollars for a chicken. Mel-
lons were sold at ten dollars, and that, when they were
rotting in superabundance. The morbid appetites of the
skeleton prisoners were taken advantage of and such prices extorted.

Trading stands were erected along the main street of
the prison. Wholesale and retail merchants operated in
divers departments, and all of them diving into the pockets of the prisoners. Tobacco was the great staple of
trade. Everybody wanted it—few could get it. Men
would barter their last shirt for it, and it is said the old,
repudiated quids were gathered and prepared for smoking. Whisky was sometimes introduced by a guard, or
an outside trader. What was denominated "a drink,"
about the fourth of a gill, cost a dollar. Such drinks
were unpopular, for experienced men declared such an allowance but an aggravation.

The prisoners made rings of bone, gutta-percha, wood,
&c., and sold them to outsiders for strong prices. Turn-
ing lathes were set up and fancy work, principally chess

men, turned, and sold at "remunerating prices." Combs, violins, earthen-ware, and many other articles were manufactured, and in a superior manner, too, and disposed of.

Some of the prisoners realized large amounts from the sale of their handiwork, and brought home with them quite a nice balance-sheet. One man is said to have saved three thousand dollars; another fifteen hundred, and many, after paying extravagantly for the necessaries of life, found a good balance left.

But contact with the rebels begat commercial demoralization among our men. Gutta-percha became scarce and valuable, and a bogus article of finger-rings was made from the horns of cattle. These, when purchased by the delighted Texan citizens, at two or three dollars, became rough and ugly on his fingers, and, finally, became brittle and broke. This was a source of outside sorrow and profanity, and brought the ring market into disrepute and suspicion.

A crockery manufacturer got up several canteens, which were much in demand among the rebel soldiers, made clay. He cast them over a tin one, and tore up an old pair of blue pants for the cover. The cloth and the strips of an old shirt, of which he made the straps, were well washed, and the clay canteens, with the piece of an old tea-pot spout for a neck, looked, as they hung in front of his quarters, like a first-rate article, and perfectly new. It was not long before a squad of rebel soldiers passed through, and were attracted by the looks of the canteens, and they were soon sold at a magnificent figure. Three months after, some of the same squad sauntered around the same quarters; and asked the manufacturer if he had any canteens for sale? Remembering his customers, he said he had not—that he did not make such things. One of the rebels, with much indignation, said they were in search of a d—d Yankee, who sold them some canteens, as they passed up, and they were nothing but clay. When they put water in them, they went to pieces. They failed to find the man who had imposed upon them.

After being imposed upon, in trading, a portion of the guards, sought their revenge by persuading some men to come to a forbidden line, and trade. When they went out to the line, and displayed their goods, they were seized by the rebels and robbed of all they had. The prisoners dared not resist, for they were in a position which would have warranted the guard in shooting them, so they had to submit, with the best grace possible.

But it was not long before they squared accounts with the rebels. When the affair seemed to be forgotten, they were invited in one night to trade. This was forbidden by the rules, but the extreme anxiety manifested by the prisoners to trade, induced the rebels to venture. As soon as business had arrived at an interesting stage, the rebels were seized, their pistols taken, and they were robbed of every moveable article about them. Their situation obliged them to submit, and they left the contraband spot, much wiser, though poorer men than before.

Exciting and amusing scenes often occurred. When a wagon ladened with produce, entered the camp, a dense crowd would gather around it. A multitude of purchasers, at a time, would so confuse the vendor, that all consciousness would be lost.

On one occasion, a pompous old planter came in with a wagon load of produce, driven by a negro. A few hundred men surrounded the wagon, at once, and made many offers to purchase. In the meantime, the lynch pins were removed, and the wheels slipped to the ends of the spindles. The hame-strings were untied, and the harness generally loosened. About that time, the planter began to suspect something wrong, and ordered his negro to drive out, quick. Jube cracked his whip, and, lo! a general catastrophy ensued. The mules slipped from the harness; the wheels rolled off; the wagon, planter, produce and negro, experienced sudden emancipation. The old gentleman felt a dozen hands in his pockets, which quickly relieved him of everything. He lost all his produce, his money, hat, harness, (for it was valuable material,) and most of his clothes, whilst his negro was carried off to the quarters, on the shoulders of the men.

Th's outrage called forth the severe denunciation from the officials ; but, upon investigation, it appearing that nobody did it, there was no punishment.

Escapes.

Though the prison was heavily guarded, escapes and attempts were of nightly occurrence. During the month of March, a party projected and completed a tunnel. It commenced inside of one of the cabins, and extended out one hundred and fifty yards beyond the stockade; but just as all was ready for a general stampede, the stockade was extended, for the accommodation of more prisoners, and the plan frustrated. This tunnel afterwards served a good purpose, for prisoners to hide in, when contemplating an escape. They would enter it and remain there until the pursuit of them outside was given up, when they would go in earnest. Several tunnels were constructed, but none were ever made available for their original purpose. One large one was within fifteen feet of completion in March, 1864, when the last but one of the prisoners of the 46th Indiana, came out. It may have been successful. It was the result of an amount of labor and ingenuity that deserved the reward of success. A shaft, six feet deep, was sunk in a cabin. The tunnel was then started towards a bank, outside, near a hundred and seventy feet distant. The chamber was two feet wide by three high. Air-holes were opened above, under a bunk or a bed, through which the miners got breath. The tools used, were case knives ; a sled, upon which was drawn out the earth in buckets, and rope made from cows tails. A station would be established midway, to which the sled would be hauled by a stationary Yankee engine. The bucket would then be put on another sled and hauled to the shaft. The first sled would, at the same time, return to the work, bearing another bucket. The earth was spread under bunks, or in holes about the camp, and covered with litter before daylight. There was a traitor among the prisoners; at last discovered to be one Hawkins, of the 120th Ohio. On discovery he was removed outside, and lived about the rebel officers' quarters, and worked for them at tailoring. On coming up the river, in March, this gentleman was thrown overboard, but was saved by the deck-hands, in their ignorance of the facts.

Nearly every movement in the camp was known to the rebel guard, and great caution was observed in laboring upon the tunnels. None but a select few knew about it. Rebel officers would come in and make a general and thorough inspection, looking especially for tunnels, of which they evidently knew something. Ramrods and swords were forced down into the earth, but no discoveries were made. The "Grand Trunk" laid too deep.

The digging of the large tunnel cost an immense amount of labor and risk. On one part of the line, the excavation had to be made fifty feet without ventilation—almost suffocating those in it.

A trained pack of hounds was constantly kept, for the purpose of tracking and hunting down fugitives from the pen, and these, were under the charge of a professional negro hunter. When a prisoner was found to have escaped, these dogs were made to take the circuit of the camp, till the track was discovered, which they would follow through the woods and swamps, and almost invariably accomplish their mission.

Music was frequently resorted to, as a blind to cover over the designs of a party meditating escape—drawing their attention by a good song, whilst a log was dug up out of the stockade, and a party, prepared for the venture were making their escape; often, within a few feet of the guards. Others, more adventurous, or desperate, would draw themselves to the top whilst a sentinel's back was turned, and quietly let themselves down upon the outside.

2

Hundreds, who had money, bribed the guards to con-
nive at their escape. Sometimes as many as twenty of a
night. The market price for such favors, was five dollars
in greenbacks. These contracts were made with men
who professed Union sentiments, and would, for money,
do the prisoners any favor in their power, when their officers were not about.

But very few, of the many who got out of the prison,
escaped. It was rare, one overcame all the dangers from
dogs, rebels, deep and swift rivers, swamps, hunger, and
the many other difficulties that beset the way to the federal lines. In from two to ten days, the fugitive was
brought back, and re-consigned to the stockade.

It was seldom the authorities discovered the absence.
of a man, escaping, until his friends made it known, or
he was re-captured. Keeping his escape a secret, gave
him a start of the hounds and cavalry, and, equal to that
in general interest, it gave the camp a ration extra.

It frequently occurred, that when a soldier died, a sailor would change clothes with the deceased, and remove
the body to his quarters. The sailor would assume his
name, get his ration and a chance for parole, or exchange,
that was never extended to the sailors.

One of the most novel and original inventions for escape, was here practiced, and with great success, for over
a month.

A prisoner under parole not to escape, drove a cart
through the camp, for the purpose of hauling the accumu-
lating dirt, to a ravine, outside. This suggested to an
Irishman, the idea of a *cartel*, perfectly feasible, and beyond the danger of interference from the regular Com-
missioners of Exchange. Two men would get into the
empty cart, over whom was thrown a blanket, or some
light brush, with the ordinary load of dirt on top. Dirt,
rubbish and Yankees, were then driven to the ravine and
tumbled down a declivity of some fifteen feet, into the
brush, when the contraband part of the load shook themselves, and hid away until darkness enabled them to leave.
The driver of the cart would dance upon his load as he

drove past the guards, as he said, to prevent suspicion; but he was suspected of doing it for his own fun as much as for any thing else.

Under this *cartel*, over a hundred and fifty men were liberated, before it was discovered by the rebels and repudiated.

Of the numbers constantly getting out, it is safe to say, that not over one in fifty escaped. The others were overtaken and brought back, to suffer the severest pains for their effort.

The nearest point in the Union lines, was at Vicksburg, a distance of three hundred miles. There was not a county in the States west of the Mississippi, within the Confederate lines, but what had a party of mounted soldiers, with a leash of trained blood-hounds, hunting deserters and conscripts. At least one-half of the population was heartily disloyal, and bearing intense hatred to Federal soldiers. An escape might well be considered a miracle.

Most of those attempting to escape, started with little or no preparation. They were ignorant of the geography of the country; with no maps nor charts. Many knew nothing about traveling at night, and were unaccustomed to traveling in forests. Their appearance would betray them to the first man they met. After a few days of bewildered wandering, exhausted by hunger and fatigue, many were obliged to barter their freedom for corn bread, and give themselves up, or more probably, be overtaken by men and hounds, and brought back. Frequently, men would travel hard all night. and by the first dawn of light, see the prison from which they had escaped, six or eight hours before. Many cases occurred, where men had reached the Mississippi. river, and were re-captured whilst hailing a gunboat or a transport. Others, within sight of the Federal pickets, would be taken by some straggling vagabond rebel band. and delivered to a post for re-conveyance to prison.

Much ingenuity was required and used to conceal the escape of a prisoner, by his comrades. Each morning, there was a general roll-call. The camp was divided into sections of from one to two hundred men. A rebel sergeant had a roll of these, and it was his duty to call the list, and ascertain the presence or absence of each man. The prisoners were formed in two ranks, and two sentinels with muskets and bayonets, passed along the front and rear of the line, as the roll was called. With all this precaution, the absent ones were duly answered · for, without discovery. Frequently, the sergeant whose duty it was to call the roll, was not able to read the names without considerable spelling, when some considerate Yankee would volunteer to assist him, and would inadvertantly miss the name of an absconding party. By universal consent, the party successfully covering up the · absence of a friend, was entitled to the surplus ration. ·

With the officers, it was more difficult than with the men. They were carried on a separate roll, but they were so successful that the name of an absent one was often carried a month, without discovery—long enough to ensure his safety.

General Treatment.

The commanding officer of Camp Ford, Lieutenant Colonel Borders, was an Englishman—a resident of the South, about nine years. From association with the most reckless and dissipated of this semi-barbarous society, he was thoroughly imbued with the worst qualities of it. By marriage, he had stepped into a fortune, and become arrogant and haughty. Here, the inate brutality of the man found full scope, and a field for cultivation. The acquisition of power, fed his pride and sharpened his malice. With all, the infamy of his character was intensified by his being a bitter rebel. A monarchist, hating everything Republican, and with unbounded malice towards the Union soldiery, he was a fit instrument to carry out the system provided by the leaders of the rebellion, of the treatment of prisoners. He had an adjutant, unprincipled, cowardly, vicious, and destitute of the dimest spark of manhood. Lieutenant Mc-Cann, was the name of this officer. He possessed no principle of action, but the slavish one of wishing to please his superiors. When some of the prisoners were coming home, through New Orleans, in March, last, this McCann was just being brought in, a prisoner. General Canby was informed of the brutality practiced by him, by Major Norris, of the 43d Indiana, when the gentleman was put in irons, and a ration of a pint of meal and a half pound of bacon was ordered for him.

If men approached too near the stockade—the limit being ten feet—they were either shot down, or made to mark time at a vigorous "double quick," at the pleasure and discretion of the sentinel ; as many of these were boys, not over fifteen years old, it was very gratifying to to the embryo traitor, to have a Yankee dance at his bidding. The inducement, a cocked musket held at the breast of a prisoner, and handled in the most reckless manner, was generally sufficient to get out of the man all the dance there was in him. Thus, a skeleton was made to jump high or low, to suit a boy's fancy.

As many as thirty at a time have been subjected to this treatment, for two hours, or until they become exhausted and fell. Confederate officers often stood by enjoying the amusing scene, and sometimes ordering a bayonet to be used in compelling men to use their feet.

Men who were overtaken in trying to escape, and returned to prison, were made to stand on blocks of wood or stumps, bare-headed in the sun for four hours, and after two hours rest, on again for "four hours." This would be continued for a week, before the man would be considered sufficiently purged of his *crime.*

Sometimes such *criminals* were made to stand half their time on one foot, whilst a soldier sat by with his musket, in some shady place to enforce obedience.

Lady visitors, (rather demons) occasionally passed around the camp to see the "animals," as they humanly termed the prisoners. Taunting them in the most insulting manner.

Groups of prisoners were often tied up by the thumbs, for some trifling offence, and suspended so that their toes barely touched the ground, and for days were brought out and subjected to this torture, two hours at a time.

Strong men subjected to this punishment in a July sun, would faint and fall as far as the ligatures on their thumbs would permit, and would be cut down as soon as a lazy, vicious rebel found it convenient to go to his assistance.

Prisoners were shot down without any attempt at justification. A man was near the gate asking to be permitted to go out for wood. The guard ordered him away. The man turned to obey the order when he was shot through the heart by the guard and killed.

A man named Colvert, of the 77th Ohio, whilst quietly walking along within the proper limits, was inhumanly shot down by a boy about fourteen years of age, who, perhaps, was ambitious of something to boast of among his associates and tutors.

S. O. Shoenicker, of the 130th Illinois, a good orderly, pious man, whilst setting in a hovel, pleading with a friend to become religious, was shot dead by a guard, some twenty yards behind him. The guard declared he had a brother who was killed in battle and " He was bound to kill some d—d —— of a —— of a Yankee."

As a punishment for this outrage, this rebel received a furlough for thirty days, which he submitted to with all grace.

A member of the 173d New York, was killed whilst walking towards the wall to obtain his hat which had been blown off. The man who committed this murder, merely remarked that he " Had killed two Yankees before—now this was three."

A member of the 36th Iowa, was shot whilst walking along the usual path, about 8 o'clock one evening. Both arms were broken, and the heart was perforated by the ball. He died in the arms of his brother, declaring he was foully murdered. This brother was paroled in March and came home.

An Indian, belonging to the 14th Kansas, was killed as wantonly as any of those above mentioned. The men who committed these outrages without rebuke, were of Colonels Sweet and Brown's battalion.

Rations and Hospital.

The regular ration consisted of a pint of corn meal, in the bran and about one pound of beef, with a little salt, to the man, but scarcely any day brought anything near the allowance. The articles issued were of the most inferior character. The meat often was not fit for use. The supply of cooking utensils was not sufficient for a battalion of men. A small allowance of wood was brought, but so meager was the supply, that a portion of the camp would have none. These having no way to cook their beef, lost it. Provisions could be bought of outsiders, but at prices beyond the reach of most of the prisoners. The officers of the camp, permitted every advantage to be taking of the starving inmates, and appeared to co-operate in creating a demand for what there was to sell.

The Hospital arrangements consisted of a new wooden building erected in the woods, near by, about large enough to accommodate thirty patients, which was about a third of the average sick, needing the most judicious treatment and close attention. Sick men, were usually, only carried out to the hospital, when it became apparent that death would soon ensue. In the hospital, the sick were on rude wooden bunks, with nothing to soften them. No blankets nor comforts of any kind, were furnished. The only advantage in the hospital over the camp, was, that the men were raised off the ground,—a gain of dryness, at the sacrifice of some comfort. The same ratios were issued to sick and well. If the sick man had a blanket, he was fortunate indeed, but if he had none, he was obliged to suffer without it. The majority laid almost naked, on rough boards and were left to get well or die as disease and his constitution determined.

The medical department was in keeping with every-thing else. A Surgeon was detailed, whose duty it was to visit the sick. He usually visited the camp about once a week, and pretended to have an inspection, but usually he came at such times as but few knew of his presence. When he was seen, he issued curses liberally, and the commonest drugs parsimoneously.

The monthly allowance of medicine to the prisoners, was not sufficient for one day's treatment of the more simple cases, and was of very inferior quality. In short, the whole thing was but a brutal and systematic farce.

Removal to Camp Groce.

On the 12th of August, five hundred and six of the prisoners were ordered to move south to Camp Groce, a distance of two hundred miles. The unfortunate ones were selected from every regiment in the camp, and made up of the unruly members of the prison community. Officers and men who had made themselves obnoxious to the officials by resisting or protesting against their infamous treatment of men held as prisoners of war, or those who had made attempts to escape.

Not over ten minutes notice was given of the proposed march. The rations of the day had not been issued, and there was nothing to be taken to eat. Rations, it was said, would follow in wagons. The line was soon formed outside, but the march was delayed many hours, whilst the men were kept in the burning sun, without water, wearying with a delay that appeared to be without cause, except for the general purpose of torturing them. John Shaffer, Jasper N. Mullins, Robert Lewis and David Garbison of the 46th Indiana, being sick and unable to make the march, were not taken.

The road, for the entire distance, ran through a pine and oak barren—extremely broken—and interspersed with narrow strips of timber, with an occasional stretch

of from five to six miles without a shrub or
scarcely a blade of grass. The sand was scorching hot,
ankle deep and with the greatest scarcity of water.
Fifteen miles frequently intervened between watering
places, where no water could be obtained for the guards
and their horses, which were always first considered.
There were not over fifty canteens among all the prisoners, and there was no way of carrying water from point
to point. The daily march was about twenty miles—ar-
ranged with a view to the water places.

In justice to the guards on this duty, it must be said
that they were the best class yet met. They belonged to
the 21st Texas, and numbered two hundred and fifty.

The intense heat, without water, caused many of the
prisoners to drop exhausted by the way-side, where they
were guarded till night came on and then forced to overtake the column. There were six or eight wagons assigned for the sick and exhausted, but they did not accommodate a fourth of the number of those utterly unable
to march. Many were without shirts—their naked backs
exposed to the sun. A large proportion were without
shoes—their feet blistering in the hot sand. Many with
their uncovered heads exposed to the almost perpen-
dicular rays of the sun.

It would be fruitless to attempt to portray the sufferings of that eleven day's march, the remembrance of
which is enough to make the heart sick.

Teams followed the column gathering rations, and often
they did not get into camp till near midnight. There was
then doled out a small cup of flour or corn-meal, and a
third of a pound of bacon to the man.

Camp Groce was at last made, when the saddest days
in the prisoner's experience commenced. There were confined in this camp, about fifty soldiers, and the officers
and crews of the gun-boats "Wave" and "Granite City,"
captured at "Calcasieu Pass" on the 6th of May, 1864,
in all, about one hundred and fifty men. They were all
sick with fever and ague. Of these, eighty died before

the following November. They were all in the most destitute condition.

This prison is about sixty miles northwest of Houston,
near Hempstead, on the Houston and Texas Central Railroad. It is situated in a sharp bend of a branch of, and
within a few miles of Brazos River. It is almost entirely
surrounded by a strip of low marshy ground, impregnat-
ing the air with a deadly malaria. About one and a half
acres of ground are enclosed with a close stockade about
twelve feet high. The prison is supplied with water from
two wells, which were found filled with rubbish and filth.
These, with great labor, were fitted for use, and furnished
a supply of slimy and unhealthy water. There were board
barracks, sufficient to accommodate six hundred and fifty
men, but in a most dilapidated condition.

The rations of this camp when the new delegation arrived were some better than in the one just left, but they
very soon contracted to uncomfortably small dimensions.

This camp was commanded by an Irish Captain, who
had been a Corporal in the regular United States Army,
and was in Texas at the breaking out of the rebellion,
when the infamous General Twiggs, so disgracefully be-
trayed his trust, and delivered up his command of trained
and disciplined soldiers, to a cowardly mob, which a volley
would have put to flight.

Of the companies of the prison guards, one was Irish ;
one German, and two were Texans. The men of the two
first were, almost to a man, as loyal as the prisoners
whom they guarded. They showed the prisoners every
possible favor and kindness, when not under the eye of
their officers. Numerous instances occurred in which
these guards after dark passed out prisoners, and even, by
means of ropes, let the prisoners down on the outside of
the stockade, and furnished them provisions for their
journey. As many as thirty in rapid succession, have gone
over the stockade on a moonlight night, either by the help
of the guard, or through their disregard of duty. These
attempts to escape were no more successful than at Camp
Ford. After wandering about the country a few days,

they were brought back, having become sick from the malaria of the country, and given themselves up, or were captured by the local force. Some died whilst out and were buried by their comrades.

The men transferred from Camp Ford, had not been long here before they began to be taken down with fevers and diarrhœa, and by the middle of September, there was not one hundred well men in the prison. The camp presented a most deplorable condition. Men crazed with fever ran hither and thither like madmen. Night and day the cries of the sick and dying filled the air. Men woke in the morning, after a night of horror to find their bunk-mates dead by their side.

No medicines were to be had until disease had become general in the camp, and many were beyond the reach of remedy. The Surgeon whose duty it was to visit the sick, but seldom came, and when he did, was drunk and administered curses in place of medicine. Many days passed without any medical attendance or relief beyond what could be furnished by the inmates of the prison. This hidious drama, was most appropriately closed by the death of the fiendish Surgeon by *delirum tremens.*

After this those who were thought too sick to be treated in camp, were carried to the Hospital at Hempstead, about two miles distant. From ten to fifteen sick men would be jammed into a wagon and carried to the Hospital over rough roads, and through the scorching sun. Four or five men died during these murderous transits and for want of room, were set or laid upon by their almost unconscious comrades.

Hospital at Hempstead.

This institutntion was the low garret of a church. The roof was almost within reach of the patients. There were no side windows—no place for ventilation but through the small gable windows. The inner view of this den was most horrible. There was but enough light to make the scene visible, and the filthy and noisome effluvia that pervaded the place, drove away all who were not forced to remain. The fresh air so greatly needed by the fevered sufferers, seemed to turn in disgust and abhorence from the threshhold of this cavern.

The sick were crowded together as thick as it was possible to wedge them—one tier over another, on rough board bunks, and generally, with no straw or mattress. If the man did not have a blanket, which was generally the case, he lay in his rags, upon the hard boards. There were a few mattresses belonging to the Hospital, but these from long use had become so foul, that they were refused by all. If the men were able to crawl down a rickety flight of stairs, the inexorable laws of nature could be complied with—otherwise comfort and cleanliness gave way to necessity.

Helpless and suffering, with fever and chronic diarrhœa, men died without thought or care. Their remains were hauled out in a cart and dumped into a hole without coffin, and without an emotion of sympathy or regret.

Change of Camp.

In September the yellow fever broke out at Galveston, and soon reached Houston and other points above. The Confederate guard at the prison, fearing the disease might reach that point, openly threatened to leave, and let the prisoners take care of themselves. On this, the authorities determined to move the camp. On the 20th, the prisoners were taken west of Brazos River, and encamped twenty-five miles from the railroad, on a low wet marshy creek bottom.

There was now five hundred men of the six hundred and fifty left. Of these there were not over seventy-five well. On the journey the sick were crowded together in rough wagons, fifteen or sixteen to a wagon. These were those only who were not able to walk. Those who the bayonet could persuade along, were obliged to go on foot. Very

few were able to walk comfortably—and a great number
got along only with the greatest difficulty. The transportation was limited and many dragging themselves along
until they could do so no longer, fell exhausted, and were
left to follow or die, or be picked up when it suited the
convenience of the guard to go back for them.

On this move six men died in the wagons, and were
hastily tumbled into holes dug by the way-side.

Sick and well alike, at this camp, had no beds but the
damp ground, and no shelter but such as they might construct with brush. They were closely packed together on
less than a half acre of ground, where the cooking and
all camp duties were performed. Sinks were dug inside
the lines, which in the hot sun rendered the atmosphere
almost unendurable. Water was obtained from pools
along the bed of the creek—green, filthy, and rank with
disease and death. As usual, above the camp the horses
of the rebels, numbering near five hundred, were kept,
watered and cleaned. The dirt of a filthy rebel camp was
intentionally thrown into the water. On the banks of the
stream were the sinks of the rebel camp. Each rain
brought down all this disgusting material, and left the
prisoners no alternative but to use that water or do without any.

Instead of the health improving, the sickness greatly
increased. There was no medicines, nor attendence of
any kind. Each morning at roll call, men were found
present in body but absent in spirit. Death had released
them. The dead would be found lying upon the ground
in the mud, having been denied the satisfaction of a bed,
and with no covering but the scanty rags that composed
their clothing. Around this few was a heavy chain of
sentinels standing guard, as it were, over a grave-yard, to
keep ghosts in subjection.

Another Move.

On the 3d of October, owing to heavy rains and cold winds, it was decreed necessary again to move the camp. A march of twenty-five miles was made near to the town of Chappel Hill. An old camp meeting ground, where were some sheds and shelter, was encamped upon. The move from the old camp, was in all respects much like tho former one, rendered worse by a more general and thorough exhaustion among the men. Now, a well man was a curiosity—none were well. As before several died in the wagons or by the road side.

The new camp, too, was located on a damp piece of ground. There was a springy ridge above it, which kept a portion of the camp constantly wet. As before no shelter was had for the prisoners, and they had the ground, only, for their beds. The cold, chilly October rains had now set in, and night after night the sad moans of the suffering; the maniacal ravings of men, delirious form fever, and the cough from hundreds of diseased lungs, sounded through and above the howling winds. Ghost-like forms crowded around cheerless fires, striving to warm their attenutated bodies, and keep in circulation the sluggish blood. And their tortures ran through many nights of pelting rain or hail.

About the 15th of Ootober, for the first time, the prison was furnished with medicines of something like an approach to decency, but still far from sufficient. A Surgeon, comparatively a humane man, abounding in good promises, of limited action and energy, was alloted to us. The health began to improve, but deaths continued at the rate of four or five a day.

There was abundant shelter for two thousand men, consisting of sheds and board houses, erected by and for the families who came for religious purposes, in times past. In these were quartered about four hundred soldiers—the guard—the rest was taken up by their horses, equipments and forage. The systematic efforts to wear out and destroy the prisoners, would have been defeated, in a measure, had they been permitted to occupy that portion of the quarters that were empty.

About the last of October, the yellow fever having subsided, the prisoners were again moved back to Camp Groce. On this journey, after having marched over four hundred miles, from the place of capture, the first railroad transportation of the campaign was furnished, and a ride of fifteen miles! as an especial favor, granted the prisoners.

The condition of the men on returning to Camp Groce, was most deplorable. There were four hundred and forty of the original number. With the exception of six or seven successful escapes, all the rest had fallen victims of the infamous treatment to which they had been subjected by the scoundrels who had charge of them.

Not one in ten of the prisoners had a hat, about one in twenty a blanket; a few had shirts; a few had pantaloons, but the majority were clothed in collections of rags that defied description, and very few had shoes.

What is known as "Northers," now occurred frequently. The suddenness of them rendered them more severe. Often with the thermometer at seventy degrees, dark clouds would start up from the northwest and in two hours the thermometer would fall to thirty five degrees. As the season advances these storms increase in frequency and intensity, and they cause more suffering than a regular season of a lower temperature.

The general misery of the prisoners' situation was greatly augmented by their inability to hear from home, or to obtain information in relation to the progress of the war. Nothing was known of the great armies of the nation—of their condition or progress. The exagerated stories of the rebels were known to be false, because unreasonable and improbable. It was known that the Red River expedition was a disasterous failure, and it was feared that like defeats had been suffered in other departments.

Nothing was heard of the regiment, but what was contained in a short letter written June 14th, by Colonel

Bringhurst, on the Mississippi, to Liutenant Colonel Flory,
as the regiment was going home on veteran furlough. At
Camp Ford, in November, a letter from Colonel B. was
received by the four members of the regiment left there
in August. It informed them that the regiment was in
Kentucky. With these exceptions, nothing was known of
the movements of the comrades of the prisoners, with
whom they had been constantly in company in camp or
field, for nearly three years.

The "Houston Telegraph" was the vehicle of the news
received by the neighborhood around Camp Groce. In it
were published the most startling accounts of Union defeats and rebel victories. Every action was a Federal
disaster, and ruin seemed constantly impending over the
National Government.

With all this, there ran through the rebel soldiery, an
anticipation of final defeat, which belied all their boasts
and predictions.

At Camp Ford on the 4th of July, the commandant of
the camp permitted the prisoners to have a celebration,
with the restriction that there was to be no allusion to
the war, or the questions at issue between the north and
south, in the speeches. Colonel Dugane, of the 75th
New York, Lieutenant Colonel Flory, of the 46th Indiana,
Captain Crocker, of the gunboat Clifton, and others made
patriotic speeches, which were highly appreciated by the
large audience. Patriotic songs were sung, and over
three hundred sat down to a 4th of July dinner, gotten
up by subscription, at the aristocratic price of $4 a ticket.

On the 8th of November, the prisoners at Camp Ford
held an election for President of the United States. The
matter was first suggested by a rebel, Colonel Brown,
then commanding the camp. He said the votes of men
coming from so many States, would indicate the result
in the actual vote. The idea was readily adopted by the
prisoners and preparations made for the important occasion. The camp was divided into wards, and persons in-
dicated, distributed slips of paper to each ward. At roll
call on the morning of the 8th, the tickets were dropped

into hats, brought together and counted. The proceeding was altogether fair. There was neither bribery, nor any undue influence used. Yet, literally, the *purity* of the ballot box, could not be fairly insisted upon.

There were 2,370 votes cast, of which 615 were cast for General McClellan, and 1,665 for Mr. Lincoln. To make the affair more closely resemble the actual proceeding, several fights among the voting sovereigns were indulged in with the usual amount of damage to the participants.

Colonel Brown was astonished at the result. He predicted the re-election of Mr. Lincoln, and declared that the chances for the success of the Confederacy, were very small. He bought three gallons of whisky, and with his officers got gloriously drunk over the "Indication."

On the 5th of December, three hundred and forty-two men and officers, including all of the 46th Indiana, present, were notified that they were to be paroled and proceed to New Orleans by way of Galveston and Houston. It did not take long to prepare for that move.

The paroled prisoners were conveyed to Galveston by railroad, where they were detained but a few hours, as a steamer was awaiting them. With some of the rebel guards, who were as glad to get away, the late prisoners were soon happy and safe under the stars and stripes.

In thirty-six hours the party was landed on the levee at New Orleans, and felt that they were again in a land of civilization.

During the voyage, John Cunningham of the 46th Indiana, died and was buried in the gulf. Isaac E. Smack and Joseph Davis, of the same regiment, died in hospital shortly after their arrival at New Orleans.

Of this regiment John Merideth died at Camp Ford, Jacob Oliver at Hempstead, and Robert Lewis and George Lane, at Camp Groce. Thomas S. Evans died on the plains, in endeavoring to escape.

Information was brought from camp Ford, by Jasper N. Mullins, who left there early in March. There were then

fifteen hundred Federal prisoners there, among them
Daniel Garbison, the only representative of the 46th.

At Shreveport, among other of different regiments,
were John Shaffer, Alexander Reed, and William Bacome.
The two latter had escaped from Camp Groce, were re-
taken and conveyed to Shreveport.

Mullins escaped from Camp Ford, by taking the place
of Enoch O'Brien, of the 43d Indiana. That regiment
was called out for parole, and as O'Brien's death which
had occurred a month before, was undiscovered, Mullins
answered to the name and was paroled.

Escape of Lieutenant Colonel Flory.

On the 13th of November, Lieutenant Colonel A. M.
Flory, of the 46th Indiana, and Captain W. B. Loring,
of the United States Navy, made preparations, having
left the prison at 4 o'clock in the afternoon.   It was the
custom of the prison commandant to give passes each
day, to Federal officers to pass out on parole, not to escape.   Upon this occasion. a pass was written by one of
these officers, who put the commandant's name to it.
With their blankets under their arms, ostensibly to collect
brush, they presented themselves at the gate, showed the
passes and were passed out.   They had previously, sent
out some Confederate clothing and some provisions. These
had been sent to a designated point.   On getting out, the
officers went to a thicket, and waited until dark, in the
mean time putting on Confederate uniforms.   At dark
they started, and traveled as rapidly and steadily as possible all night.   It is estimated they made between thirty
and thirty-five miles, which is all that saved them.   The
escape was discovered the next morning, and cavalry sent
in the direction they had taken, but the cavalry did not
make that day, the distance the officers did the night before, and gave up the chase.   The fugitives did not stop
long the morning after the escape.   After a half hour's
rest and a cup of coffee, they again pushed on and in

twenty-four hours after leaving prison, they were fifty-five miles away, with twenty miles of swamp between them and their pursuers. They were then on the head waters of the San Jacinto, and in a perfect wilderness.

This description of country extends a distance of one hundred miles, without the sign of a habitation. The region is traversed by the San Jacinto, Trinity and Neches Rivers, with their numerous tributaries, and is covered with heavy timber and dense cane-brakes, matted with brambles and every kind of tangled growth, common to the rich alluvial soil of the south. Heavy pine forests lay across the track, hundreds of acres of which, had fallen from the effects of fire, forming a most intricate abatis, grown up with an immense growth of blackberry briers, often ten or twelve f.et high, and under ordinary circumstances, impenetrable. The fugitives were obliged for many rods, to cut their way through these jungles with a knife, and then pass into a cane-brake of enormous growth, equally laborious and discouraging. Passing these there would be a stream to cross, which had to be swam, again to enter upon the like experience upon the other side.

Thus they traveled day by day, with food in their haversacks to tempt them, but it must last ten days. The stock, twelve pounds of flour bread, two pounds of bacon, a little coffee and sugar, must hold out until cultivated districts are reached.

On the 20th they crossed the Neches River—quite a considerable stream. Heavy rains having prevailed for two days the entire country was, in a manner flooded— the streams full and the bottoms overflowed.

Owing to the cloudy weather they were now unable to travel for two days. Having no compass, it was impossible to keep the direction in a wilderness without the sun or stars.

Again, occasionally getting a glimpse of the sun, and by the aid of the clouds the fugitives marched on. At last. food all gone—hungry and drenched with rain—they reached a corn-field—the limit of civilization. They at

once fill:d their haversacks with corn, built a fire in the
woods, and on a tin plate cooked their grated corn-meal.

Having reached a part of the country where discovery
was possible, they prepared for night marching   At dark
they started guided by the moon, and made the greatest
distance possible by morning   They had water to wade,
bayous to swim, and tangled cane-brakes to penetrate.
About the 25th a cold norther sprung up, and ice froze a
quarter of an inch thick.   Struggling through this was
laborious and discouraging.

As the travelers approached the eastern line of Texas,
which is the Sabine River, they became entangled in
bayous, which form a perfect net work.   Scarcely had
they crossed one before another presented itself.   For two
nights they marched hard without, as it afterwards was
learned, making any material advance.   Coming at length
to a saw-mill, they discovered a negro in a boat.   They
secreted themselves in the brush until dark, when stealing
cautiously up, they captured the boat and quietly drifted
out into the bayou.   When out of hearing they rowed
down the stream.   Down this bayou they moved until 3
o'clock in the morning, when coming to a larger one running south, they imagined themselves in the Sabine River.
Crossing this they landed, set the boat adrift and took an
eastern course through a dense cypress forest.   The sky
being overcast with clouds, they had no guide for direction.   After three hours march in day light, they were
astonished to find fresh tracks, and came to the conclusion that they were followed, but on examination they
proved to be their own tracks, and they discovered they
were not two hundred yards from where they landed.
That day's march was made through briars and swamps.
Three times they were compelled to build rafts, undress
and swim streams, two of which were full a hundred and
fifty yards wide, swift and very cold.   Three times during that day, they crossed their own path; it being almost
impossible to keep direction—getting only an occasional
glimpse of the sun, during intervals of rain.

Night found them on a plain traveled road, which after a good rest, they followed all night, wading mud and water and swimming a very wide cold stream. At day-light they entered a dense woods, built a fire and parched and eat their last grain of corn.

They took the road again near night, and coming to a dilapidated hut, learned from a woman that they had passed during the night, the road they should have taken. A retreat was necessary, and at dark they found the road and stopped at a house for the night. Here the party got a good supper, bed and breakfast, and discovered, after a careful course of questions, that instead of being across the Sabine and out of Texas, they were on the west side of that river, and but five miles from where they set out thirty-six hours before.

Early next day the river was reached and crossed on a table turned bottom up. Now there was no mistake, and the fugitives had to be prepared for bold movements. They had prepared before starting, orders with the signature of the Colonel of a Texas regiment, directing them to go to their homes near Vermillionville, Louisiana, to remount, and refit. The order stated that their horses had died, and the men were out of clothes. It was the intention now to push on boldly, as rebel soldiers. As such, they successfully passed Niblett's Bluff, through the fortification, eat dinner with the rebels, and handled the "Vandal Yankees" without mercy. Here, incidentally, they gathered all needful information in regard to stopping places on the road.

They were now forty-five miles from "Lake Charles," the most dangerous point on the route, where a number of escaped men had been re-captured and sent back.

On the evening of the 30th, they reached the "City," crossed boldly at the ferry and lodged with the ferryman, at whose house there was a squad of Provost guards. Their papers were examined, and pronounced good. On the morning of the 1st of December, they rode in the wagon of their host, which took them twelve miles on the road, and with a letter of introduction to a friend of his,

who lived some twenty miles beyond. Here again they
enjoyed the hospitality due the soldier.

On the 2d they traveled hard over a low flat prairie,
covered with water and met the most dangerous adven-
ture of the trip. A Confederate Colonel, stationed at
Lake Charles, met the fugitives on the road, and with a
musket presented, demanded their papers. They were
handed over and closely examined. He deliberately gave
it as his opinion, that the party were escaped Yankees,
and that their papers were forgeries. This insult was re-
sented in a becoming manner, but it required very close
management, and skillful talking to convince the Colonel
that they were really Louisiana soldiers going home on
leave, to refit. This, however, was done, and the mag-
nanimous Colonel, attoned for his unjust suspicions by
putting his own endorsement on the paper. This made
the paper perfectly good, up to the point it specified.

Approaching Vermillionville, it was deemed more safe
to travel at night and lie by all day. There were Confederate troops at every station, and on the road, and the
danger would be increasing as they came nearer the
Union lines.

After marching the first night until 4 o'clock in the
morning, a heavy rain came on. They waited until light
and discovered a wood about a mile distant. Here they
determined to remain all day, but found the wood to be
but a narrow strip of oak, with no underbrush, a house
on either side not twenty rods off, and with the scene not
improved by a negro riding from one house to the other.
Being almost discovered by the negro, and most probably
seen from one of the houses, they were forced to come
out. They found an officer at home on leave, and two
rebel soldiers on furlough. The clothes of the fugitives
were soaking wet, and they were most frozen, as a norther
had come with daylight. The rebels made them welcome
and gave them hot coffee, and seats at a large fire. They
remained until after dinner, and were treated with the
greatest kindness.

A rebel Government wagon train going east, was overtaken and they rode in it till night.

The night of the 3d of December, near Vermillionville, the officers passed in the woods where the regiment of Lieutenant Colonel Flory encamped the year before. The party was now safe as regarded the road, for Colonel Flory had been over it three times.

They had now eighty miles to the lines, and traveled at night hiding by day and living on parched corn. They meet squads of rebels on the road, but would turn off as soon as they would hear them. They passed around the towns, and had no further trouble before reaching Berwick Bay, on the night of the 7th of December. A gunboat lying in the stream was hailed, but no boat was sent over until morning, when they were taken on board the boat, the most completely overjoyed men that it is possible to conceive of. Their Confederate rags were soon stripped off and suits of navy blue given them. They were once again under the stars and stripes, and almost bowed with reverence as they gazed on the old flag, and felt its protecting power.

In twenty-five days these officers traveled five hundred miles, swam over twenty streams pushing their clothing before them on rafts; for twenty days they were in the water almost constantly, and for days had nothing to eat but corn.

Escape of Carr and Guess.

Joseph Car and Jacob Guess, escaped from the stockade at Camp Groce, on the night of the 3d of September. A good singer of the 130th Illinois, who frequently performed this part, was employed in attracting the attention of the guard by a song. When singing was going on, the guards would collect in the neighborhood and enjoy the music, with the prisoners. The fugitives climbed the stockade and traveled to the very best of their abilities, until daylight, and made twenty-five miles. It was necessary to make a good stretch the first night to get clear of the dogs.

All the next day they laid in a prairie near a town. The sun was very hot and they obtained but little rest. The next night, they made a good march, but were very much fatigued. On the third night they came to and crossed the San Jacinto river, and passed through an immense cane-brake. On the other side, was a cornfield, from which they obtained some roasting ears.

On the morning after, they found themselves, after a laborious night's march, surrounded by a settlement. They retraced their steps, and made a detour around the settlement. It was not deemed safe to proceed, so they laid by all day, but three or four hundred yards from a house on either side of them, and between which, negroes with dogs, frequently passed. During the next night they came to the railroad, near Trinity river. Whilst passing a plantation house, they were attacked by dogs, which alarmed and brought out the proprietor. They asked for water, when the man began to ask suspicious questions, which scared the travelers, and they pushed on. Carr subsequently learned that this man was an ardent sympathiser with escaping prisoners, and he would have assisted them, had they remained long enough to have satisfied him that they were Union soldiers.

Carr and his companion then struck a line of posts, as they really were, fifteen, twenty-four, and twenty miles apart, of Union people, with whom they rested and recruited, after their night's march.

At one of these places, the man being from home, the woman directed the men where to hide, and then sent them food. She told them if they would remain another day, she would prepare them a quantity of provisions, and send them some clothing, of which, she saw they were in the greatest need. They remained, for both were sick and weary, and the next day a friendly Irishman brought them out enough clothing to make them comfortable, and good provisions.

They were now six days out, and Guess had become so sick, that he was unable to proceed. He went to a neighboring house, declared himself an escaped prisoner, and was taken back to the stockade, from Beaumont, on the train.

Carr went on alone, traveling during the night, and lying by or near a friendly house during the day.

The stations were upon the railroad, and were kept by other than Southern people. They directed escaping prisoners from one to the other. One station beyond the Sabine, ended the friendly route. ·Here, when fifteen days from camp, Carr had become very sick, and was obliged to halt. He had been lying out in the woods during the day, and staying in the house at night. He could not be kept in the house during the day, because of the hands at work on the road. He became rapidly worse, and determined to give himself up. The man who had been taking care of him, took him on a hand-car, back to Beaumont, twenty-five miles. Here Carr went to a friendly house, but finding that he could not be concealed, directed the proprietor to go to the military commandant, and inform him that an escaped prisoner had just come there, sick. Carr was arrested, and taken in a boat down to Sabine City, to the Hospital. He became very ill, and remained there four weeks. He was then put in the guard house.

There being a fleet of Federal vessels in the bay, Carr wrote, under a flag of truce, to the Commandant, stating the situation of himself and another prisoner, and asking for some clothes. After some delay, a boat, under a flag of truce, brought up a package, containing a splendid suit of seaman's clothing, for each of the prisoners, embracing every article required for a complete suit. A letter accompanied the goods, stating that they were the gift of the officers and men of the U. S. ship "Pocahontas."

Subsequently, Carr's shoes were stolen by the guard—afterwards his stockings and overcoat.

After being in the guard house five weeks, and being
perfectly recovered, Carr was sent back to the stockade,
and making his appearance in his fine clothes, was received with hearty shouts.

Escape of Dennis Bagley.

Bagley escaped from the stockade on the evening of
October 15th. He took a wrong direction, and was seen
by a negro wading a river. The unusual circumstance,
was reported by the negro, to his master, who told some
home guards, and Bagley was followed, and arrested
whilst resting upon a log. He was returned to the stockade the next day, almost before he was missed.

Another opportunity offering, on the night of the 16th
of November, Bagley again went out, with William Cook
of the 46th, and a member of the 34th Indiana.

They traveled nearly east, and met with good success,
until they came to the Sabine, where they were seen and
suspected. They were halted at Sibley's Bluff, where, as
three men arresting them, went into a house, Bagley ran
off and escaped. His comrades were captured.

The next day, Bagley was fairly captured at "Lake
Charles," where he was securely locked up in prison.
After six days' confinement, with others, he was taken
towards Alexandria. When within forty miles of their
destination, a dance was gotten up, one evening, at the
camp fire, by some of the Federal prisoners, and Bagley
and a member of a Missouri regiment, took advantage of
the inattention of the guards, and left without them.
The escaped men traveled all night, and were not overtaken. They kept on at nights, and, passing near China-
ville, came along the Red River road. At one place,
they came, unexpectedly, upon a negro in the woods.
He knew what they were, and assured them he would not
expose them. After getting them food, he got a horse,
and piloted them twelve miles. Subsequently, when
they heard chopping in the woods, they would go directly
to the negroes, and obtain food and advice from them.

At "Lake Charles," Bagley heard of Lieutenant Colonel Flory and his companion. The officer who had met them, had become convinced that he had been imposed upon. He was exceedingly angry with the success of the Yankees, and with his own stupidity.

The travelers crossed the numerous bayous on the road and, finally, struck the Atchafalya. The great width of this stream, for a time, baffled them, but they got over.

They were now within a day's march of the Mississippi, and began to feel extremely anxious and fearful. On the east side of the Atchafalya, they stopped to get breakfast at a house on the road-side. They passed for Confederate soldiers, and were invited to sit down to breakfast. The proprietor had been a heavy sufferer from our army, in its repeated marches past there. On the return down Red River, the soldiers had taken every horse he had, with much other property. He waxed wroth in relating the outrages practiced upon him by the Yankees. The fugitives became alarmed at his vindictive utterances, and thought themselves discovered. The breakfast they were eating, was disposed of very rapidly, and they were glad to find themselves again on the outside. There is no question, but what the man knew who his guests were, and was only prevented from going into them by prudential considerations.

The next day, December 16th, brought the wanderers to Morganza, where they were once more under the flag that could protect them.

Death of Thos. S. Evans.

In August, about thirty men of the 46th Indiana, escaped from the stockade at Camp Groce. They scaled the walls, early, one bright moonlight night, unobserved, whilst a party of singers drew the attention of the guards in another direction. After getting outside, the men separated into squads of two to four, and took different directions. One of these squads was made up of

William Bacome and Thos. Smith Evans.' These traveled hard during the night, and laid by during the day.
After crossing the San Jacinto river, they entered a wilderness region of country, in width, from twenty to forty
miles, and extending to the Sabine river, the eastern
boundary of the State,—a wild, uninhabited desert,—
abounding in marshes and jungles. Upon getting some
forty miles into this wilderness, both men were taken sick.
Their rations became exhausted,. and after wandering
about some days, hunting for a settlement, or a habitation, in vain, were obliged to halt, from weakness. Evans
became delirious from brain fever, and Bacome, under
the effects of fever and ague, was unable to assist Evans,
or in any way to alleviate his sufferings.

In this deplorable condition, in the midst of a desert,
infested with wild animals, muttering around them by
day, and howling by night, with no hope, they looked for
a horrible death. During the day, Bacome would roam
over the wilderness, attempting to find even an unfriend-
ly house, and return at night, unsuccessful. Daylight
would again find him on the same errand, to meet with
the same disappointment, and to pass a terrible night
with his suffering and sinking companion.

Four days, he passed in this way, but found no sign of
a habitation, or the sight or sound of a human being.
He chose to remain with his companion until he died,
rather than to seek his own safety by deserting him to
the beasts that were about. At last, Evans died, alone,
with his suffering and helpless, but faithful friend, with
the howl of the wolf, the last sound that fell upon his
ear.

Bacome dug a grave, as well as he could, in his weak
state, with sticks; buried his friend, and then only,
thought of his own safety.

Almost unable to travel, Bacome nerved himself for
a desperate attempt to reach a habitation. After traveling a distance of twenty miles, through cane-brakes and
swamps; almost impenetrable forests; miles of fallen

timber, overgrown with brambles, he gave himself up. He was kindly treated until he recovered sufficiently to return to the prison.

This sad story, when related at the camp, cast a gloom over the prisoners. Evans was a good soldier, and much respected by his comrades.

Bacome again escaped, in a few weeks, and was not heard of until in March, when hearing that J. N. Mullens, one of his regiment, was at Shreveport, on his way home, he sent him a line, stating that he was in prison, near Shreveport.

Other Escapes.

In addition to the escapes already narrated, there were numerous others. Of these, but one, so far as is known, was successful. Lawrence Hartlerode, who left Camp Groce on the night of the 4th, and reached the Union lines on the 21st of September. He left the prison at a time when some forty escaped. They divided into small parties, but were all re-taken, with the above exception, at various times, and on different stages of the journey.

Of the 46th, who were so unlucky, were Moses Tucker, Ellis Hughs, Alex. Reed, John Briggs, Theo. Taylor, Geo. Oden, Isaac E. Smack, David Murphy, John T. Reese, Elihu Shaffer, Geo. W. Nield, T. C. Jackson and Anthony Eskew.

Tucker, Hughs, Briggs, Reed and Taylor, went together on the night of the big escape. Tucker gave up in two or three days, Briggs and Taylor were brought back in a few days, and then Hughs and Reed.

Oden, in company with two men from another regiment, got nearly to the Sabine, but becoming sick, had to give up. They were taken to Houston and put in jail,—again moved and put in a jail, where Oden was when the regiment left Camp Groce. He was, subsequently, paroled.

Smack, Murphy, Reese and Jackson, met with the usual run of ill-luck, and one fine day found themselves back in Camp Groce.

Nield and Eskew were lost sight of, shortly after they escaped. Nield has never been heard of, nor anything positive about Eskew.

Shaffer escaped with Hartlerode, and was with him several days; they became separated, and Shaffer being sick, was obliged to give himself up.

Jenkins, passed for a man of the 46th Indiana, who was dead, and was paroled as one of that regiment at Camp Ford.

Colcasieu Bay Expedition.

In April, 1864, an expedition of four transports and gunboats, was sent from New Orleans up the Sabine Pass, into Calcasieu Bay, for cotton, cattle, &c. There accompanied the fleet, a squad of thirty-seven men, from the "non-veteran" camp at Algiers, under the charge of a Lieutenant of the 30th Maine.

The fleet had arrived in the Bay, and whilst two of the boats were below, the others, the "Wave" and "Granite City," whilst lying without steam, and no proper guard, and with the infantry on the opposite shore, were furiously attacked, at daybreak, one morning, by a force with a battery, from Sabine City.

The boats were not iron clad, and were exposed, helpless and unmanageable, to the rebels, concealed along the bank. After a short but sharp conflict, the two boats surrendered.

The infantry, on shore, had taken no part in the conflict, and might have, for the present, at least, escaped; but through mismanagement on the part of the officer in command, they were surrendered.

Among these prisoners, were Maxwell Reece, R. V. McDowell, Hugh Quinn, Joshua T. Colvin, Phillip M. Benjamin and Jacob Oliver, "non-veterans" of the 46th Indiana.

The infantry, and the officers and crews of the boats, were taken to Sabine City, and thence, to Camp Groce, where they were met by the Red River delegation in August.

The boats captured, were hid, for awhile, in Sabine River, but were afterwards engaged in the rebel service, and, subsequently destroyed.

But little was said about this unfortunate affair, and it will, probably, never be known, for whose benefit the sacrifice was made.

The Loss.

Of the 46th Regiment, Indiana Veteran Volunteers, at the battle of Mansfield, April 8, 1864 :

KILLED.

Lieut. Jacob Hudlow,	Private Jas. A. Hastings,
" John McClung,	" Wm. R. Clouse,
Private Archibald Smock,	" Thos. W. Scott,
" Geo. Hunsinger,	" Hiram Lombart,
" Jacob II. Cripliver,	" Edgar Folk.

WOUNDED.

Capt. Wm. M. Pigman,	Private Terrence Dunn,
" Frank Swigart,	" John McTaggart,
Sergt. Jos. Henderson,	" Samuel Cree,
" Geo. W. Yeates,	" Johnson Lidgard,
Corp. David Bishop,	" Jeff. Marshman.
Private Michael Blue, ·	" Porter A. White,

PRISONERS.

Lieutenant Colonel A. M. FLORY.
Captain WILLIAM M. D'HART.
Chaplain H. ROBB.

Sergeant David Murphy,
"   Wm. Bacome,
"   Geo. W. Nield,
"   Ellis J. Hughs,
"   John Shaffer,
"   George Huffman,
"   Jos. H. Carr,
"   J. N. Mullins,
"   Cyrus J. Peabody,
"   John A Wilson,
"   John Vanmeter.
Corporal Lewis Canter,
"   John W. Castle,
"   Thos. S. Evans,
"   Herman Hebner,
"   M. McConnahay,
"   Theo. Taylor,
"   Jonathan Hiney,
"   Bradley Porter,
"   D. C. Jenkens,
"   Jesse Shamp.
Private Levi Canter,
"   John W. Creson,
"   John T. Reese,
"   J. R. Cunningham,
"   Joseph Davis,
"   Henry Grant,
"   Geo. W. Oden,
"   Benj. F. Shelley,
"   John R. Shields,
"   Anthony Babeno,
"   Geo. Lane,
"   Robert Lewis,
"   John Sheppard,
"   Isaac E. Smack,
"   Anthony A. Eskew,
"   James H. Gardiner,

Private William H. Small,
"   Lewis Baer,
"   John W. Briggs,
"   Henry Itskin,
"   James McBeth,
"   Alex. Reid,
"   Chas. T. Rider,
"   Moses M. Tucker,
"   John W. Welch,
"   Jas. Coleman,
"   Samuel Gable,
"   Jacob Gates,
"   John Meredith,
"   Jacob Sell,
"   Dennis Bagley,
"   J. C. Chamberlin,
"   Jacob Guess,
"   Wm. Hayward,
"   Allen White,
"   John B. Walden,
"   Jas. Fisher,
"   Dan. Garbison.
"   Law. Hartlerode,
"   Jas. Passons,
"   Amos Orput,
"   John Hamilton,
"   George Sleh,
"   Wm. Cook,
"   Sam. Johnson,
"   Wm. Kreigbaum,
"   Geo. W. Mathews,
"   Ambrose McVoke,
"   George Moore,
"   Elihu Shaffer,
"   Elmore Shelt,
"   John Stallard,
"   Wm. Fahler.

AWAY DOWN IN TEXAS

—DURING THE—

GREAT REBELLION!

—OR—

An account of thrilling interest.

The Experiences, Adventures and ultimate
Fate of a number of Cass and Pulaski
County Boys.

———

THE 46th INDIANA VETERANS WITH GENERAL BAN

Dodging the Rebels.

—:o:—

What an interesting volume might be given to the work, were all the adventures, romantic episodes and thrilling incidents of the late civil war placed in the hands of some ready, graphic writer, to be woven into graceful narritive. Who does not love to linger over the dashing heroism and fine patriotism of the Revolutionary Fathers? The simplest account or story of that glorious epoch never fails to entrance and interest the American readers. So will it be in the future, as each glowing chapter of the mighty struggle between patriotism and treason emerges into the light and falls into the hands of posterity. The war of the Centaurs, the heroism of the Trojans, the glorious triumphs of the Grecians may be sang in enrapturing measures; but no age, era, no triumphant march of conquest and glory can ever enter the heart of impulsive glory. America as do the pages of the history of the "Great Rebellion," and he who will take pains and delight in snatching even but one short paragraph thereof from obscurity and oblivion, will gain for himself a warm place in the heart and memory of the patriotic sons and daughters of our great and prosperous republic.

We are about to undertake this pleasant task, in giving the adventures and terrible experience of a brave and worthy soldier friend and acquaintance—one with whom many of our readers enjoy a very pleasant and intimate acquaintanceship. True, our hero was but an humble private in the rank and file, but our narrative will prove him to be worthy of the highest honor and respect, and his record as brilliant as that of many a glory-crowned chief and epauletted officer.

LAWRENCE H. RTLERODE was born in Champaign county, Ohio, 1842. Until the breaking out of the late war he pursued the humble and manotonous life of a farmer. In 1861 he was quietly engaged at his avocation on a farm, about three miles south-east of Winamac, in Pulaski county,

Indiana, whither he had moved a few years previous. As with the hundreds of thousands of those who cast their all—their fortunes, their sacred homes, and their lives in defense of the nation's integrity—the soul-stirring music of the Union was too much for this patriotic heart; the call for brave arms to strike in behalf of the nation's honor was too pleading and touching in its nature to resist, and he promptly took a place in the ranks of enthusiastic and patriotic volunteers. He enlisted in Company H., 46th Regiment Indiana Veterans. Dr. F. B. Thomas, of Winamac, was their original Captain. The Company was attached to the 46th Indiana, then under command of Col. G. N. Fitch, of Logansport. Most of the Regiment was made up of brave young men from this section of the State, all of whom won many glorious laurels during their long and dangerous term of service, and those who survived the dreadful contest, returned home to receive a joyful and deeply grateful welcome from the hearts and hands of their beloved "home ones." Many of them are still with us, dearly honored and respected for the glorious part they took in the great work of our country's salvation, and while they live may they ever prove worthy of the grand laurels that encircle them, so that after death the same glorious truths, increased in brilliancy and warmth, may crown their memories while the noble government which they preserved shall exist to keep them hallowed and sacred.

We shall not attempt to follow the Regiment in its varied course, as its history is given in the preceeding pages of a truthful and graceful pen. If you, dear reader, have perused the work this far, you have already learned that our hero (and the regiment of which he was a member) found it his lot to bear an important part in the memorable Banks' Expedition, on the Red River, Texas. You have heard how he, in company with a large number of others, was taken prisoner; how they were driven from one filthy prison pen to another; the terrible sufferings and outrages that they were forced to endure; of their final escape and of the sad fate of all of them, excepting Mr. Hartlerode, who, after a long, painful and almost fatal journey on foot, hiding and skulking for safety in marshes and forests during the day, and causiously plodding his way, with bleeding, blistered and bruised feet, and nude limbs, during the night time, evidently succeeded in gaining the welcome Union lines. Dwell on the thought—fleeing from tortures severer than those of the rack and pillory—pursued by blood hounds, whose shrill and blood-thirsty baying smote his ears as he tremblingly hastened toward home and friends, dreading and shrinking momentarily for fear that their sharp fangs would seize his quivering flesh; his bare feet leaving their imprints in blood upon the wild soil; his legs lacerated and torn by sharp briars and brushes; his clothes torn to shreds by the thick undergrowth; his tongue hot and swollen for want of cool, refreshing water; his body reduced to a skeleton, pale, weak and emaciated from cruel and worse than savage starvation! Think of this sad wretch of what was, but a short time previous, a hale, happy, enthusiastic, brave Union soldier, hiding, grooping his way through a trackless wild, living on roots and berries, swimming filthy, slimy, reptile-infested streams, and pursued all the while by hungry hounds and sought after by men whose hearts seemed to be still more savage and cruel, if possible, than the nature of the fierce and irrational brutes that obeyed their friendish commands! Does the contemplation not fill you with horror, kindness, and, at the same time, is not your love and admiration for the devotion and unyielding patriotism of the Union soldier greatly increased and strengthened? Surely, no one can peruse such a picture without having his admiration for devoted patriotism and self-sacrificing heroism wonderfully magnified.

The Rebel Prison.

Our narrative opens in a close, filthy rebel prison, at Camp Groce, Texas, on the morning of September 4th, 1864. A number of the poor, half-starved, shivering victims had clustered together, as if to strengthen and support each other by close contact, when they were approached by one of the prison guards, who was a "Union man" at heart, but who was doing guard duty in the vile service, having been forced into the rebel ranks. He pitied the wretched prisoners, and, it seems, he had been busy and on the alert for some time concocting some plan for their relief and escape. At length his plans were matured, and now he approaches the cluster of "boys" that have just attracted our attention, to quietly communicate to them the welcome secret, for a secret it had to be, and a deadly one, too, it proved to be, to many a one who was unfortunate enough to let it "slip" or become known to the prison keepers. He reveals the time, place and manner of escape, and gives the necessary instructions for caution and action. Who can imagine the feelings of joy and hope that were awakened in each patriotic heart on receiving this happy intelligence, in grasping hold of this frail straw, as it were, of deliverance! Ah, the bright visions of home and dreams that shone in their hearts were no doubt warm and sincere; but, alas, how many never realized their fond dreams! Only one of that band of truly wretched, forlorn prisoners ever tasted of the sweet realities of the hope awakened by that friend's kind news, or

"Breathed the air again
Of their freedom and their own beloved home."

As usual, the pint of corn meal and a little rock salt was served to the famished beings, and right heartily did they set about its preparation. Never did food taste better than it did upon that memorable occasion, for the hope that it would be the last meal of that kind, and in that place, increased its palatableness, and also diminished considerably the wanted time occupied in its preparation and cooking. What a long, long day it seemed to be. The hours hung long and painful as the mind worried and struggled with anxiety and dread, anxious for the appointed hour to arrive, and fearful but the suspicious, watchful eye of some one of the beastly guards would detect their plans and frustrate their designs! Many were the anxious, silent, but very expressive and well-understood looks that were exchanged among the eager band during that weary, anxious day. How much can be communicated by a silent look or expression of countenance, especially among those whose hearts are in deep, earnest sympathy and accord! Finally the shades of twilight began to lower over the scene, wrapping friend and foe alike in its dusky embrace and completely obliterating all lines and features of difference, making the foe unknown and indistinguishable to his

aggressor, and casting its mystic silent spell over all.
Nearer and nearer came the appointed moment, and faster
and faster beat and throbbed rhe excited, anxious hearts!
At last the signal was given; the way was clear; the gateway
was guarded by a friend, whose tongue was sealed and
dumb while the forty refugees silently and cautiously
emerged from the filthy, pestilential enclosure, determined
to regain home and freedom again, if human endurance,
aided by a kind providence, could possibly do so. At this
hour the officials were less vigilant than usual, making the
chance for escape more opening, although the country surrounding the camp was very forbidding to an escape at
that hour of the night, which was the cause of the accustomed lack of vigilance at that time. It was far distant to
a town or human habitation; a great expansion of prairie
land extended far and near, rendering flight very hazard-
ous and laborious, almost too much for mortal persons to
triumph over, unless, as in this instance, life and freedom were the precious rewards held up to the gaze of the
struggling one or crowned the happy victors.

After passing, and silently, sadly and grately glancing
a last farewell to the friendly guard,—a friend in disguise,
who had done so much for them—can the finite mind ever
imagine or idealize the emotions, the thoughts of those
forty men as they stood outside of the hated stockade
walls, deliverance and freedom lying away beyond, with
untold suffering and privations and hundreds of wearisome,
savage wilds between, and captivity, torture and almost
certain death threatening them within the enclosure from
which they had just escaped, and to which a thoughtless
whisper or unguarded foot-fall might momentarily recog-
nize them! There they stood, bewildered by the sudden
transposition, hardly knowing how to proceed; how to over-
come the mighty obstacles that faced them so boldly. Men
accustomed to hardships and daring, however, do not dwell
long in hesitancy and doubt. "Let us regain the Union
lines!" was the unanimous and speedy conclusion, and
then came the solemn moment when these cowards in suffering, marches, battle and imprisonment had to separate;
bid each other farewell; a sad, a last farewell! No time
was to be lost, and tearfully they grasped each others
hand, stammering out the sad, short words of separation,

In the fifth line from the bottom read "comrades" for "cowards."

then scattered to the many points of the compass, three
and four in a squad, trusting to the great Deliverer for
safety and success, for they had no friendly guide to lead;
no trusty needle to point the way; no sign or mark to show
the way through the trackless wilds; nothing but their
own judgments to guide and direct them!

The squad which we shall follow was made up of Lawrence Hartlerode, Isaac E, Smack, David Murphy and
Elihu Shaffer. This quartette chose Brashear City, Lous-
iana, as their destination, which was distant about three
hundred miles. The first thing to do on setting out, was
to make an effort to baffle the blood hounds, which they
feared would be set upon their trail, immediately on the
discovery of their escape. They happily succeeded in this
important advantage by traveling over the prairie on the
first night. Heavy dews fall upon the prairie and low
lands in that section of country during the night, which
are quickly dispelled in the morning by the glorious sun,
completely obliterating any trail or track that may have
been made in the night time, so that the hounds could not
trace them far, or their escape being discovered in the
morning; which, fortunately, did not occur until a pretty
late hour. This step was, indeed, considered on the part
of the fugitives, and was, no doubt, the cause of their escape. In the timber a trail remained traceable to the
hounds for forty-eight hours, it is said. This would have
been a very unfavorable condition of things for our heroes,
and well was it that they bethought themselves of the great
advantages of which they so happily and successfully
availed themselves. Thirty miles were traveled the first
night, showing the energy of hope and the power of determination. On the second night the pint of corn meal was
exhausted. Then a new and serious embarrassment stared
them in the face. They could travel with bare and sore
feet and tired legs through marsh and jungle and over
rough and hard surfaces, but how could life hold out without food to replace the exhausted muscle and worn-out
bones and sinews? The second day was spent in a fruitless
tramp, and just as evening began to close around they came
up to a corn field. How beautiful this field of golden maize
appeared, almost supernaturally so, because it just then
brought success to their weakened and failing bodies. A

good quantity of corn was speedily parched, and was, no
doubt, devoured with as much gusto as were the sweet
potatoes by the patriotic Marion in the presence of the
visiting young British officer. The field also contained
a certain kind of black pea, which the party endeavored to
cook, but the time for departure came before the peas were
sufficiently boiled. They attempted to eat the undone
food, but their stomachs proved too weak to digest the
coarse substance, and it was left to mark their resting
place. A dark gloomy night was now before them, and
their course led through a jungly forest and a thick cane-
brake swamp. As might be expected, they lost their way
in this savage waste. After wandering about for some
time, all hope of further progress that night forsook them,
and, completely tired out, they sank down to rest in this
dark habitation of wild animals. Nothing but the light of
Omnicence could look in upon! How many such lonely,
sad, darkly-enshrouded pictures the Eye of Heaven be-
holds! The next morning on awakening they found their
beds of earth resting beneath two inches of water. No
trouble for them to wash their faces, which they did, and
again set out upon their journey. Soon they brought up
on the bank of the Nachess river. After following it up
stream for about half a mile, they crossed to the opposite
side, carrying their clothing upon their heads. Some time
in the afternoon they came upon a party of negroes, who
were engaged in the manufacture of salt. They had some
of their rock salt left yet, which they exchanged with the
negroes for some of their finer product. The negroes said
their masters were rebels. The boys asked them to tell no
one of their passing along in that locality, assuring them
that they were on their way to fight for the freedom of all
the colored people in the land. But little progress was
made in that night's travel, owing to the tangled wild
through which they passed. About two o'clock in the
morning they came upon some water in a pool, in which
swine had been wallowing the day previous. Every drop
was eagerly drank by them, they being nearly famished,
having had no water for many preceeding hours. How
great must be the sufferings of one driven to such an extreme straight! It is only in such terrible predicaments
that we learn to know our insignificance, and the great

love of the Creator toward us in strengthening our powers
of endurance and affording us timely relief. Here a halt
was made to enjoy a few moment's rest. On preparing to
resume their journey, Isaac E. Smack fell over, apparently
lifeless! Here was new and frightful trouble! To think
that one of their number had to be left dead in that doleful
region, was enough to madden their already over-wearied
minds. In their anxiety they fell to rubbing the prostrate
fellow, and were soon delighted to see signs of resuscitation.
He soon became conscious, but was unable to travel. After leading him slowly along for about two miles, they were
forced to stop with him. Here they remained until day
dawned, when, happily, a house was discovered not far distant. Mr. Smack went to the house, while the remaining
trio continued on their weary line of march. But a few
grains of their parched corn yet remained at this time, and
they began anxiously to look and search about for further
supplies. Many deer and black bear abounded all about
them, but they unfortunately had not the means wherewith
to capture them. The trials of Tantalus were nothing
compared to this, surely! Just think of it—large numbers of sleek, fat bear and deer dancing and prancing all
around you—yet the pangs of starvation keep gnawing at
your stomachs, driving you almost to desperation, and no
power to relieve yourself. There our little party put in
another whole night of weary, fruitless travel. Morning
came, but the onward movement was kept up at as rapid
rate as possible under the circumstances. About twelve
o'clock in the day a house appeared in the distance, but
they feared to approach it, lest it might prove the resort of
foes and they be re-captured. Here David Murphy began
to complain of feeling very sick, and he too was compelled
to linger by the wayside, fixing himself as well as he could
in the woods to await the result of his illness. The band
was now reduced to a duad. A friendly corn field here
favored the fugitives with a further supply of food. They
profited by laying in a liberal amount. After several days
and nights of tedious, weary journeying, they reached the
Sabine river. A small town marked this point. Here a
boat was pressed into service, by which the opposite side
of the river was gained. Three or four hours were spent in
endeavoring to cross a broad swamp, but the sickle-grass

and young cane, being eight feet high and standing as thick as could be, proved too much of a barrier. Retracing their steps to the river, they built a fire upon its bank and remained at rest until morning. Again setting forth, they proceeded but a short distance up the river, when they struck an old road. Following this, they were led through the swamp, which was about three miles wide, with ease. Leaving this untraveled road, they soon approached a very deep stream, the banks of which were filled with alligators. The vicious animals plunged into the water at the approach of the intruders upon their solitude. Perhaps no more loathsome or abhorent spectacle ever greeted human vision than that offered by a large number of these unsightly, voracious animals in a body, lazily enjoying themselves in some wild and marshy locality. We have beheld the sights upon several occasions, and we cannot recall the instance without horror and shuddering. Here, indeed, was another serious difficulty for our friends to surmount. The depth of the stream was itself a great obstacle to the passage thereof, but how was a crossing to be made in the midst of such a horde of ferocious reptiles! Fortunately, a lot of old telegraph poles was lying near at hand. Several of these were rolled into the stream and lashed together with grass, thus extemporizing a raft, on which to carry the haversacks, clothing, etc., to the opposite side. Shaffer swam before and pulled, and Hartlerode pushed in the rear. Imagine their feelings when their naked legs came in contact with some object! Alligators! no doubt thrilled along every nerve filiment in their bodies, and caused them to leap and shriek in terror! Thus days and nights were spent in perilous and exhausting travel, until at last Shaffer became sick and was scarcely able to move along. A halt was made. After parching the usual meal of corn, Hartlerode procured some boneset and made a tea for his sick comrade. The decoction had the effect of temporarily invigorating Shaffer, enabling him to resume the journey. They were about ten miles from Lake Charles when Shaffer declared that he could go no further. A house chanced to be in view at the time and thither the twain nearly dragged themselves. They found it occupied by a woman and several children. They informed her that they were escaped yankee prisoners; that they were sick, tired and hungry, and that they were desirous to give themselves up. She gave them permission to remain, and appeared to be greatly pleased. She said her husband was a Captain and had command of Lake Charles, and that they could go over and see him in the morning. She then set about preparing supper, which she announced was in readiness in a very few minutes. Each place at the table was furnished with a plate, a knife, and a tin full of water. In the center of the table was a large dish filled with well prepared hominy. This was, indeed, a RECHERCHE dish for the exhausted fugitives, and right heartily did they partake of it. A short time after supper they were shown to bed. The couch was a small "trundle bed," such as are occupied by our children. It was too short by several feet for the new occupants. Nevertheless the tired, worn-out men soon fell into deep, sweet sleep upon its easy bosom. During the night a large cat annoyed Hartlerode. He put the impudent creature off the bed several times in a gentle manner. It still persisted in returning until his patience was exhausted, when he seized it and hurled it violently against the wall. It troubled him no more after that. The travelers felt considerably recuperated in the morning after a hearty supper, a good night's rest and a capital breakfast on water and hominy, they were ferried across a stream by a lad, who directed them in a road to Lake Charles. As soon as they were out of sight, however, they pursued their course northward in the direction of their destination. Shaffer had improved greatly on the fare of the last twelve hours, and the two journeyed onward with renewed hopes and energies. They soon came upon another stream. Here they made a raft out of brush and placed their clothing and what little baggage they had upon it. After crossing the river, they were in sight of Lake Charles. Being tired and hungry, they now stopped, built a fire and parched their corn, their daily food. On resuming their journey, they passed along to the left of the lake, continuing to travel all night. The next day, about two o'clock in the afternoon, they came to a very pretty fine grove, situated upon the bosom of a lovely prairie. The spot seemed so inviting and pleasant that they concluded to take a good rest beneath the cool and refreshing shade of the grove. The first thing in order was to sleep. Shaffer chose his bed near a

path that meandered through the woods. Hartlerode re-
monstrated against the idea of falling asleep so near the
pathway, fearing that some one might pass along and dis-
cover them. Of course, their capture would have been
easy, especially if they had been come upon while asleep.
Hartlerode, therefore, chose a resting place several rods
distant from the path. Little did he dream on laying down
to take that sleep, that on awakening thereupon he should
find himself solitary and alone, deserted by his comrade,
toward whom he had been so kind and faithful, and who
had shared with him the perils and sufferings of the long,
tiresome journey thus far! Perfidy is base and infernal at
all times, but when it shows its gorgon head in a boon companion, one in whom we have placed confidence, and who
we cherished and rated above all others, it becomes inde-
scribably cruel and contemptible! A few moments after
laying down, Hartlerode was locked fast in a deep, sound
sleep. Whether Shaffer allowed himself to go to sleep we
know not. All we know is, that after sleeping soundly for
several hours, Mr. H. awoke, jumped to his feet and proceeded to arouse his, as he supposed sleeping companion,
when, MIRABILE! he was gone! Imagine the thoughts and
feelings of the lone man! What had become of his companion? Had he been carried off? After a little deliberation,
this did not appear at all probable. He too would surely
have been discovered in his close proximity, had there been
an enemy there! Then the suspicion of DESERTION, aye,
TREASON, entered his mind. He called loudly, but no an-
swer came from the savage solitude, not even an echo to
his own trembling, forlorn voice! Alone, and about one
hundred and twenty-five miles distant from the lines of the
Union army, without food and no raiment, only a few rags
upon his person, is it at all surprising that he broke down,
and gave vent to his despondency in hot, bitter tears!
Shaffer had taken all the salt and matches with him, so that
the solitary refugee had not even the means to season and
cook his food or warm his naked, shivering body! He soon
collected himself, however, and after a little search he discovered the foot-prints of his false-hearted comrade. He
started in hot pursuit, entertaining a faint hope that he
might perhaps overtake him. Thus was an eager squad of
four reduced to one despondent, almost desperate plodder.

About sunset he came upon a highway, and then too he
discovered the crooked tracks of the deserter. Onward he
hastened until he became exhausted, but still no Shaffer
appeared to view, far out-distancing his pursuer, he being a
very rapid walker. All night the lonely, sorely stricken
Hartlerode jogged slowly along as best he could, keeping
the road. Just at daylight he discovered where Shaffer had
left the highway. He took the same direction, traveling
as briskly as he could. In the evening he struck the road
again, and, lo, there was Shaffer's tracks plainly discerni-
ble once more! About three o'clock in the afternoon, or
morning rather, he reached Vermillionville, Louisiana, and
on the suburbs of that town he lost all traces of Shaffer.
As he lost sight of the deserter's last tracks, be assured he
sent no blessings after the heartless, faithless one, nor can
he ever recall his name without feelings of disgust and con-
tempt. Hartlerode had slept none since deserted by his
companion, and had lived on sweet potatoes alone. He
passed around the town, and on gaining the road again,
about a mile beyond, so exhausted was he that he fell prostrated by the road-side and went to sleep. On awakening
and regaining his feet, he discovered a guard but a short
distance ahead, guarding a pontoon bridge across Vermillion Bayou. He unobservedly gained the bank and passed
down several hundred yards, when he crossed over. Several horses were hitched at this point, which fact suggested
to our hero the propriety of making as speedy and quiet a
decampment of the place as was practicable and possible.
A twenty-two mile prairie now spread itself out before our
journier, across which he proceeded to tread his way wear-
ily. About eight o'clock he espied a horseman approaching at a galloping rate. Here was a serious dilemma! Was
the rider a friend or foe? Prudence is always the better
part of valor, so thought Hartlerode at that moment at
least. He quickly threw himself upon the ground and rapidly rolled his body over and over for about fifty yards and
crawled into a cluster of hazel brush, crouching as low as
possible. The horseman rode up to the spot where he had
observed the figure of a man and stopped, looking all about
him. Then he started, looking and searching closely on
every hand, evidently deeply perplexed about the myste-
rious, if not to him miraculous, disappearance of what he no.

doubt felt certain was a man. He carried an Enfield rifle, which he, without a doubt, would have called into dreadful service had he discovered the crouching, trembling, almost naked fugitive. The heart of the poor soldier must have throbbed hot and violently in his throat as he momentarily expected to be discovered. How hard it must have seemed, after all the terrible sufferings endured, to be shot like a low dog on that desolate prairie, there to die and rot unknown, lost for all time to the knowledge of his dear ones at home! Can there be severer pain than the terrible pangs experienced at such awful moments? We think not. Sweet was the deeply drawn sigh and breath of relief our hero breathed when he beheld the dreaded rider disappear in the distance, and lengthy and rapid were the strides he made to get a safer locality. An old house soon appeared, to which he repaired. It was vacant and dilapidated. Two planks laid in the loft. He drew them together and made a bed thereon. Here he rested the remainder of the day, without food or water, his supply of sweet potatoes having been exhausted. At dark he resumed his tramp, pursuing his way unmolested until he reached a point within three or four miles of New Iberia, where he met a party of rebel soldiery under command of a Colonel. A number of wagons were following after. Here was another ordeal to pass through. There was no time to deliberate or lay plans. The emergency had to be met right off, and that most boldly. On coming up, the officer stopped, which was the signal for his whole command to halt. Hartlerode addressed him first, accosting him with a loose, jolly bravado.

"Good night, Colonel."

The officer responded dryly:—

"Good night."

Hartlerode inquired, in the same presumptuous manner:—

"Where are you going this time of night?" to which the officer replied:

"We are falling back!"

"What's the matter?" persisted Hartlerode.

"The yank's are coming up again," replied the Colonel, moving on as if fearful of an attack. He then asked Hartlerode where he was going, he replying that he was bound for Franklin, a town about twenty-five miles distant. He then demanded his name, Hartlerode giving him his proper name. The next question was:—

"Where have you been?"

Hartlerode told him that he had been confined in prison for a long time, and was now on his way home for some rest and clothing.

"What regiment do you belong to?" was next asked.

"General Green's old regiment," was the reply. This was a rebel regiment, with which Hartlerode was acquainted in Texas, the most of the members thereof, thanks to good fortune, being citizens of the county or parish in which this colloquy was taking place.

"Oh, yes; I know some of the boys in that regiment," and the Colonel moved on, telling Hartlerode that he had better hurry on home, or the yanks would beat him there.

"I'll conceal myself until they pass through," he replied. "Oh, yes," were the last words of the Colonel, to which Hartlerode gayly responded:—"Good night, Colonel!"

The rebel soldiers were jubilant and frolicsome as he passed them, some yelling "How are you, Sam," they taking him for a negro, so begrimmed and filthy was he in appearance. Thus was this dilemma happily and safely passed, and he pursued his way in better spirits, hoping soon to meet the "yankees," his friends and brothers-in-arms. In this he was disappointed, however. He reached Franklin about four o'clock in the morning, passing on the right of the town through the woods, travelling very slowly and cautiously. On and still on he plodded his tedious way, about prostrated with hunger, for five days and nights had passed without anything to eat but a few raw sweet potatoes. One night he met a negro on a gray horse, and after saluting him, entreated him for something to eat, assuring him that he was almost starved to death. The negro declared that he could give him nothing, as he could not possibly get food for his own family. Hartlerode then told him that he had suffered a long and cruel imprisonment; that he was a Union soldier, and that he was now endeavoring to reach his home again. His sad story aroused the sympathies of the colored man. He jumped from his horse and thoroughly surveyed the traveler. When he saw that the legs of his pantaloons and the sleeves of his coat and shirt were completely worn and torn off, that the balance

of his raiment was nothing but filthy rags, and that his
body was lacerated and bleeding, the effects of thorns,
brush &c., through which he had traveled, the negro could
resist the plea no longer, and he invited Hartlerode to go
with him. He led the way to a large oak tree not far distant and told him to remain there under it until he returned. Fearing that he might deceive or betray him,
Hartlerode placed himself in a position so that he could
observe his movements. His cabin was not far off, and
soon the stove began to rattle. This welcome sound had
the effect of allaying all fears and suspicions in Hartlerode's mind, and he returned to the tree as directed and
patiently awaited the return of the negro. In about an
hour and a half he made his appearance with a huge piece
of piping, smoking hot sweet corn-bread, three or four
pounds of fresh beef and some sweet potatoes, and cheer-
fully bade the worn, hungry soldier to partake thereof.
Never was a meal more heartily relished, or partaken of
with deeper, sincerer gratitude. After finishing his meal,
the negro carefully packed the food that was left and insisted
on Hartlerode taking it with him, declaring that he had
plenty for himself and family. When Hartlerode gave the
colored man good-bye, he wept like a child, expressing his
determination to accompany him. He had formed in his
own mind many glorious castles and had painted many sub-
lime pictures of the
           "Happy land of freedom"
Away up in the North, and he had now, once for all, re-
solved to go to that happy domain. Hartlerode advised
him to remain with his family a little longer, telling him
that the negroes would soon all be set at liberty, and that he
could take his family with him then. This pacified him
somewhat, but the tears were still flowing as Hartlerode
gave him good-bye, and set out upon his journey. The
next important point gained was Patterson. A detach-
ment of rebel soldiers was quartered here. There was no
way to pass but directly through the town. Here was truly
another serious difficulty to surmount. How to do it successfully, was the perplexing question. An old railroad
grade passed directly through the place, and the side
ditches were filled with a tall, rank growth of sickle-grass.
Here was an opportunity, a severe and tedious one, how-

ever. The severity of ordeals has no terror to those who
are struggling for "dear life." "Is there a CHANCE for me
to survive, if I pass through it?" is the only question asked
by the victims. Hartlerode was quick to avail himself of
this only chance of escape and safe passage through the
town. Down in the ditch he got, and crawled on his hands
and knees through the sharp, knife-like sickle-grass for a
distance of three-fourths of a mile, all the while within
speaking distance of the enemy. The passage was successfully made, however, a grand triumph of perseverance and
determination. A while before he had marched proudly
and victoriously through the enemies' land, now he was
stealing out of it on his hands and knees, almost as naked
as at his birth, and nearly as weak and helpless from starvation. The severe toil, the deep gashes cut by the sharp
grass, and the terrible feelings of anxiety and fear that rent
and convulsed him, caused the sweat to pour from his fore-
head, but, thank God, when he sprang to his feet HE STOOD
BEYOND THE ENEMIES' LINES! He wiped the sweat from his
face (and can we not safely say there were tears of joy com-
mingled with it?) within the lines of the glorious Union
army. What a great degree of hate must have accompanied his last look back over the country through which he
had thus crawled, crouched and suffered, marking his
course with his life-blood for hundreds of miles! Can we
blame him if bitter imprecations dropped from his lips almost at the same moment that the prayer of joy and gratitude for his deliverance was breathed forth? Surely not.
But a few miles intervened now between him and the Union
army. Be assured they were as speedily traversed as his
wounded and tired limbs could carry him. Can any one
imagine what his feelings were on entering the Union camp
once again. after such a long and painful absence! True,
he was not approaching and joining his old comrades and
acquaintances. those with whom he had enlisted and
fought and from whose midst the cruel fate of war had torn
him, but he knew that he was amid friends, brothers-in-
arms, who were there to defend and fight for the integri-
of the same glorious Union. the same beloved country, f
which he had suffered and endured so much. Thou;
wearing the appearance of a dirty savage, he was most cc
dially welcomed by the soldiers whom he joined. He h

nothing on his body at all to hide his nakedness but a small filthy rag about the pelvis, and his body was literally lacerated and cut to pieces, huge drops of blood trickling down from the deep gashes. Surely such an object of pity would call forth the warmest sympathies and generosity from even the most disinterested heart, especially when the deplorable condition was brought about in the patriotic defense of our loved land.

From the dire effects of this long and terrible tramp, Mr. Hartlerode has as not yet recovered, nor is it at all possible that he ever will fully recover therefrom. After his rejoining the army nothing remarkable occurred during the balance of his term of enlistment, which he served out, that is worthy of notice above that of the many thousands who served with him in the ranks. What we have written concerning his escape from prison and the terrible sufferings and daring adventures of his lengthy and obscure route of escape, we caught from his own tongue and from his intimate friends and acquaintances. In personal address, Mr. Hartlerode is pleasing. In stature he is ordinary, complexion and hair light, voice weak and speech faltering, cast of features sharp, demeanor quiet and unassuming, and his morals are above reproach or question. We have passed his quiet little home, situated about three miles south-west of Winamac, Indiana, where he now resides, several times, and judge from the orderly arrangement of outward things about his home, that he lives comfortably and happy. No doubt he has spent many an interesting hour with his little family in recounting to them portions of the thrilling narrative we have attempted to give in the preceeding pages, with the hope of interesting many kind readers. May our hero live long and may just honors ever be shown him for the noble part he played in the great tragedy—THE PRESERVATION OF THE UNION!

Little need be said of the fate of the three comrades who fell by the wayside. Smack, the first to fail fell into the hands of the rebels at the house he sought shelter, the occupants being rebels. He remained at the house for several days and was then taken back to Camp Groce, where he remained until paroled. Murphy was more fortunate in that the occupants of the house where he stopped proved to be Union people, who treated him very kindly. He re

mained with them for five days, when he felt strong enough
to resume his journey, but just as he was about to start, a
squad of rebel soldiers chanced to come up, who, of course,
took him prisoner. He too was returned to Camp Groce,
where he remained until paroled. Shaffer, the deserter,
after travelling several days, his guilty conscience no doubt
preying heavily upon him, became wholly discouraged and
prostrated. He proceeded to a house that chanced to be
on his route, occupied by a rebel family, and here gave
himself up to the rebel authorities, and was also returned
to Camp Groce, where he remained until paroled.

www.ingramcontent.com/pod-product-compliance
Lightning Source LLC
Chambersburg PA
CBHW022145090426
42742CB00010B/1394

* 9 7 8 3 7 4 4 7 5 9 2 7 4 *